To Joanne,

I hope you enjoy the book... and it was a pleasure meeting you!

Bob Mathers

3/12/25

To Jeanne,

I hope you enjoy the book... and it was a pleasure meeting you!

— Bob Matson

1975
AN INCREDIBLE JOURNEY

Bob Mathers

Copyright © 2025 by Bob Mathers

All rights reserved.

No portion of this book may be reproduced in any form without written permission from the publisher or author, except as permitted by U.S. copyright law.

This publication is designed to provide accurate and authoritative information in regard to the subject matter covered. It is sold with the understanding that neither the author nor the publisher is engaged in rendering legal, investment, accounting or other professional services. While the publisher and author have used their best efforts in preparing this book, they make no representations or warranties with respect to the accuracy or completeness of the contents of this book and specifically disclaim any implied warranties of merchantability or fitness for a particular purpose. No warranty may be created or extended by sales representatives or written sales materials. The advice and strategies contained herein may not be suitable for your situation. You should consult with a professional when appropriate. Neither the publisher nor the author shall be liable for any loss of profit or any other commercial damages, including but not limited to special, incidental, consequential, personal, or other damages.

ISBN Paper Back:979-8-9922613-2-5

ISBN Hardcover: 979-8-9922613-3-2

1st edition 2025

DEDICATION

To my Lord and Savior Jesus Christ, who, apart from Him, I can accomplish nothing.

Frank and Loucel Mathers, 1975

The Mathers Siblings. Lynda, Walt, Gail, and Me.

ACKNOWLEDGMENTS

I would like to thank my wife Elaine for her support through the years. She's a good-intentioned woman who loves the Lord.

Appreciation as well to friends and colleagues who read varying portions of the manuscript and provided advice and feedback. My family for sure. The Lord saved all of us. Four of the six have gone home. My sister Gail and I remain. My best to the many friends who encouraged me to first write the book, and then to keep on going with it until completion.

I would like to thank radio folks like Bruce Holberg, Ken Merson, Jack Edwards, and Jerry Danoff (Daniels) (WCBM Baltimore), Al Frazier (WSUX Seaford), and Brian Calvert (KOMO Seattle) who in the years following my return to civilian life...either directly or indirectly...inspired me to learn and grow as a radio person.

Larry Clark from the WPOC days, who, in spite of my irresponsible ways, trained me well in spite of it all. And then there were the likes of Buddy Deane and Jack Gale, two of the most accomplished personalities in the history of broadcasting. Cherished friends. Deeply missed.

A big thanks to the National Personnel Records Center in Missouri, who provided me with a one-inch thick package of my Military History which helped me to establish an accurate timeline of events related to this book.

Most of all, I thank the Good Lord Jesus Christ. He has shepherded me through more than a few hazardous waters over the years. Hard to believe it's been a half-century since this all happened. I didn't even have a personal relationship with Christ during this time, but He was patiently working His plan drawing me ever nearer...and His mercy and grace extended to me throughout my life is beyond appreciating.

Contents

Chapter One 1
   SETTING THE FOUNDATION

CHAPTER Two 7
   MURIEL

Chapter Three 13
   WORKING DAYS AND HEADY NIGHTS

Chapter Four 21
   WELCOME TO LACKLAND

Chapter Five 29
   BASIC TRAINING

Chapter Six 39
   SHEPPARD DAYS

Chapter Seven 49
   HOME ON LEAVE

Chapter Eight 55
   TURKISH WAKE UP CALL

Chapter Nine 63
   GOING UP THE CHAIN

Chapter Ten 71
   COME FLY WITH ME

Chapter Eleven 79
   WELCOME TO NEW YORK

Chapter Twelve 87
   WE'RE HERE. NOW WHAT?

Chapter Thirteen 95
   ALMOST BUT NOT QUITE LIKE OLD TIMES

Chapter Fourteen 105
   YES SIR, DOVER AND OUT

Chapter Fifteen 117
    LIFE WITH LINNIS AND ON THE MOVE

Chapter Sixteen 125
    THE SIDEWALKS OF NEW YORK

Chapter Seventeen 131
    A CAMEO AT FORT HAMILTON131

Chapter Eighteen 141
    BACK IN TURKEY

Chapter Nineteen 149
    A BREAK IN THE ACTION

Chapter Twenty 157
    BACK IN BALTIMORE

Chapter Twenty-one 165
    WORKING THROUGH THE SADNESS

CHAPTER Twenty-two 173
    Adios Baltimore, Hello Incirlik

Chapter Twenty-three 181
    SPIRALING DOWNWARD

CHAPTER Twenty-four 189
    ONE MORE HURDLE

Chapter Twenty-five 197
    MCGUIRE AND DONE

Chapter Twenty-six 203
    Epilogue
    About the Author 211

Bob Mathers, May 1975.

PREFACE

I've told this story to many people over the years, and they have found it of some interest. It is a recounting of my Air Force days that produced some bizarre and unbelievable events. The story in many respects is not really important to most people, but I lived it, and it is a time of my life that for no other reason than putting it on the record, I feel led to tell it.

To the casual observer, military service is not exceptional unless the actions produce heroism, valor, and the supreme sacrifice.

I wholeheartedly agree with bestowing honor on such events. As a man who is now in his mid-60s living in the mid-2020s, our servicemen and women are even more deserving of support. The United States of America, as of this writing, is under a relentless attack from forces who seek to destroy our constitution, end our freedoms, and subject this God-blessed land to the authority of evil-minded people.

May the Lord have mercy on America.

Even as a young boy of 16 in late 1974, I loved our country and was raised on patriotism and the flag.

Thus, the decision was made to enlist in the U.S. Air Force. For several reasons.

My father and brother were both Navy vets. Dad served on the Intrepid under Admiral William F. Halsey from 1942-46. Walt landed on the CVA-62 U.S.S. Independence. He was in 1967-71. It seemed normal to me at the time to join the military and pursue an opportunity to build a foundation and learn a specific skill.

In my case, the foundation was broadcasting. Our family didn't have money for college then. Grants were available, but I had neither the patience nor the focus to apply. The military and its promise of immediate paid training were more attractive.

So, the enlistment papers were signed just after my 17th birthday in December of '74, and on 10 February 1975, I boarded the plane to San Antonio, and down to Lackland Air Force Base we went.

For the next 13 months, my military experience was anything but normal.

Before we further tell the story, I wish to apologize in advance to anyone reading this tale who may come away offended. Perhaps there are some who might think I am romanticizing my actions in the year we're about to cover. Trust me when I say it is anything but an ode to yours truly.

This story is more appropriate from the perspective of God's mercy on an impulsive and immature young man who at any number of stops along this odyssey, escaped serious prosecution and perhaps even death from decisions made in that summer of 1975.

Here's hoping you like the book.

Bob Mathers

December 25, 2021.

A one-year-old Bob Mathers honing in on his lifelong career choice.

530 Park Avenue
New York 21, N.Y.
26 May 1959

Mr. Frank Mathers
510 South Brunswick Street
Baltimore, Md.

Dear Mathers:

    Thank you for your telegram.

    All the best to you and my namesake.

                                Cordially yours,

                                W. F. HALSEY
                                Fleet Admiral
                                U.S. Navy (Retired)

FADM W.F. HALSEY, USN (Ret.)
530 Park Avenue
New York 21, N.Y.

                Mr. Frank Mathers

                    510 South Brunswick Street

                        Baltimore. Md.

A 1959 letter from Navy Admiral William F. Halsey thanking Dad for naming me after him.

CHAPTER ONE

SETTING THE FOUNDATION

It is the case that with anything we do in life, decisions have consequences. My formative years laid the groundwork for what was to come in 1975. In some cases, good, and in some, maybe not so good.

From the time I was a kid, I wanted to be on the radio. Older family members claim from the time I was 9 months old, I could read. This all started when they noticed I was particularly attracted to commercials on TV. My brother Walt is the caretaker of family history, and he says about little brother Bob, 'you would waddle into the living room, stand in front of the TV and watch the commercials, and then waddle out of the room when the shows came back on'.

My father explained how I was able to determine my ability to read at such an early age.

'You would stand up in your playpen when TV commercials came on, point at specific commercials as they were playing, and mumble. You couldn't talk then, so it was gibberish. But you seemed to do it with just certain ones. So, one day I wrote on a piece of paper 6 or 7 names of products that got your attention. Names like Frigidaire, Kelvinator, Westinghouse, and Philco.'

'I would say to you, "Show me Frigidaire," and you would point to the word Frigidaire. You did it with all of the others, every time pointing to the word I would say.'

I could read newspapers at the age of three. Both Dad and Grandpop would take me to the local bar in blue-collar southwest Baltimore and bet an unsuspecting patron a beer that this little fellow sitting on a stool could read the headline. Every time, they got the beer, and I got a Coke.

Elementary school was easy. When I started in kindergarten in the fall of '62, I would soon be asked to read Golden Books to my classmates. My teachers made fun of me, and the other kids didn't particularly like that. So, I got challenged to fight more than I would have otherwise.

I never liked conflict, so in an effort to be 'one of the crowds,' I dumbed myself down. Instead of applying myself to be all that I could be, Bob figured goofing off would prove to classmates that he was just a regular guy.

By the time elementary school ended in the spring of '69, I was blessed through the devoted efforts of my school counselor, Mrs. Vesta Copeland. She took a shine to me and procured not one, not two, but four scholarship choices to the finest private schools in Baltimore.

I chose The Park School. When classes began in September of that year, the culture shock was soon too much for me to handle. I went from poor, non-descript, working class southwest Baltimore to the privileged, millionaire, chauffeur-driven lifestyle of classmates whose parents included the owner of the Baltimore Orioles (Jerry Hoffberger) and the famous head of the Harvey Meyerhoff construction empire. Pete Hoffberger and Jack Meyerhoff were regular kids. We got along pretty well, but I feared them finding out my social status.

Plus, the irresponsible and lazy efforts I put forth in my last years of elementary school were soon exposed to teachers there who couldn't understand why a kid with such intelligence was so stupid in his actions. Remember, in an effort to gain acceptance with the other kids, I mailed it in. That came back to haunt me in short order.

Thus, as I gathered lower grades and appeared to be about as shy and backward as they come, I quit after just 30 days and went back to public school. An impulsive decision to say the least. In retrospect, those kids would have been astounded at what I could have produced and never looked at my humble circumstances as anything other than an inspiration.

Publicly I was relieved. Inside I felt like a failure. This was a failure entering the tender teen years that not only did I own, it in turn owned me for years to come.

We resumed our coasting routine and struggled through two years of an accelerated course at Rock Glen Junior High. My main memory from those years was the overcrowded student body that found me going to school in the 8th grade from 8 AM until noon.

A mere 4 hours in the morning, and then out every afternoon to run the streets and play around. Loved it.

Then it was on to one of four brand new schools opening in Baltimore in the fall of 1971. Southwestern was just blocks from my house. No bus rides. Walked back and forth every day. I did 4 years in 3 and graduated from there in the 11th grade. That was not really an accomplishment, per se. Baltimore city schools by the early 70s were really dumbed down. All you had to do was show up, and they would pass you.

However, I did take an interest in two subjects in my last year of high school. Constance Whiteley's journalism course and Joe Press' radio and TV repair class.

It was at this point in my life that the tide began to turn for yours truly.

Miss Whiteley was passionate about writing and proper story structure. So much so that she gave me extra essay assignments and I soaked them up like a sponge. The more she gave, the more I did.

I went to Mr. Press in my senior year in the Fall of 1973 at Southwestern High School and told him I never cared much for fixing radios or TV's. He asked me if I would like to help him build a closed-circuit radio station to play records to the kids in the cafeteria. Now THAT got my attention, and I was disk jockey every day to the kids.

Writing stories and being a disk jockey. I never missed much time in my last year of school (in the 10th grade, I hooked many classes and large stretches of time), because school was now stimulating and fun!

The high school diploma came in May of '74. Like Alice Cooper said in those days, school's out, for summer, and in this case, forever.

Or so I thought. A whole 'mother type of learning experience was waiting just round the bend.

1975: An Incredible Journey

Muriel, the lovely young lass who stole my heart.

CHAPTER TWO

MURIEL

I've always said that each of us is a walking book. Of course, most of us feel that no one except for maybe you or me and a few other people would have any interest in reading the story of our lives.

In my case, I am hoping the detours and digressions set down in this book that mention people, places, and events have some relevancy to the main motivation for penning this memoir. That is, the incredible events of August 5-September 2, 1975, involving my rather idealistic efforts to right a perceived wrong bestowed upon me by the administrative arm of the United States Air Force. Plus, the events that followed after that. They're all pulled up out of history in all of their inexplicable developments.

We'll get to all of that in due time. Right now, our recall goes back to the sultry, steamy Baltimore summer of 1974. That season went by rather fast, except for one rather fascinating occurrence.

Back in the summer of '69, at the age of 11, I walked out onto the back porch of 506 Brunswick Street. Turning to look down the back alley about three houses down was a rather cute girl who got my attention.

Muriel McCartney was at that time all of 9 years old. I was 11. Puppy love struck that day. Due to her very strict mother (which was a good thing), Muriel and her identical twin sister Dena were not allowed to leave the yard. To compound the challenge, their 3-year-old brother Paul was too smart for his own good and was most dutiful in reporting back to Mom any untoward conversation or action between the two of us.

I was able to tell the girls apart in that Muriel wore pink-framed cat-eye glasses and her sister donned blue-framed specs. My close friend Rick Thomas accompanied me on many of these forays down the alley, and he liked Dena as a friend, although Dena was hoping for a stronger engagement.

Then again, when you're 11 and 9, what kind of 'engagement' are we really talking about here? Spin the bottle? Yes, we actually had a good session of that going one day before Paul reported in to Mother with his observations, and that event, of course, came to a screeching halt.

Their mother was also named Muriel. A very pretty lady who was, from my pre-teen perspective, a woman to be respected if not feared. About a year later, the family moved to a modest row house on adjacent Dulany Street. There was a small alley between their house at 2613 Dulany and the one next door at 2615.

One day, Rick, Dena, Muriel, and I were standing at the side fence of the house when the girls were called inside, and then their mom emerged to tell us to stay away from her daughters.

Rick and I sheepishly walked away, and after talking about this development, we decided to execute a plan that was designed to get the girls' attention and let them know we were still thinking about them.

We went down to the red store on Dulany and East Lynn Avenue and bought a dozen eggs. Then we walked back up the hill to their house.

The eggs were not intended for consumption. Rick and I figured we'd toss them against the side of the house, landing a couple of notable splats against the window and door. As my buddy and I congratulated ourselves on the completion of our project, we heard approaching footsteps and a loud voice.

We turned to look, and there was a frightening sight. Miss Muriel was 15 yards behind and closing fast. She had intentions of dismemberment or worse. Immediately, Rick and I took off in different directions, but she had me in her sights for some reason and stayed on my trail.

A quick right turns into the back alley and just ahead, a pipe leading up to the roof of a one-storey garage. I began shinnying up that pipe. When I ascended, I looked down and behind, and Mom Muriel had started up as well.

She quickly decided she wasn't of a mind to climb roofs on that sunny day. So, she stopped, and with a look that meant business, proceeded to tell me to stay away from her, her house, and all adjoining property. Forever.

I took her seriously. So much so that shortly thereafter, I came through the side alley one day and noticed they had moved.

That was Summer 1970.

Time went by. The grandmother (also named Muriel) and her husband continued to live at 500 Brunswick Street, but there were no visits from my heartthrob and her family. I figured that period was over, and they would never be seen again.

Then, four years later, I walked out of the front of the house and looked three doors down, and voila! There they were again! The twins!

Now, Muriel is 14 years old, and seeing her at this point with her tall, willowy frame and even more cuteness having developed into a young woman from a gangly kid made quite an impression on me. One that stayed with me for a long time.

We talked a bit, and she shared they were staying with family friends in east Baltimore while a new house was completing construction in Edgewood, Maryland, a small suburban community 25 miles northeast of Baltimore. I told her to let me know when she got settled because I wanted to talk to her again and then gave her my phone number.

Then Mom came out with Dad. The girls had to leave. Mom gave me a withering look (pretty mean, to say the least), but I didn't pay that much mind. It was Muriel who, sitting in the car as it pulled away, was staring at me and smiling hugely. That picture burned into my brain. She couldn't have left a more lasting impression.

This encounter was, as far as I can recall, around the 4th of July in '74. The emotional fireworks stayed with me all summer. It didn't matter whether I went to Wildwood, New Jersey, or to Baltimore's Inner Harbor; she was with me everywhere I went. In my thoughts.

Then one day in August, I got a phone call from the object of my long-distance affections. Her parents had to go back to the old house for a few days and renovate the place for sale. They left the girls at the family friend's house. 3135 Fait Avenue. The home of Doug and Honey Sessa. The voice on the line was Muriel's, asking if Rick and I would like to come over and hang out.

Rick was up for it. We rode our ten speeds over (neither one of us owned a car at that time) five miles through city traffic and spent the day with Muriel and Dena. When it got dark, we headed back across town. In between, we walked the neighborhood, having nice conversations, and I was feeling pretty happy. To say the least.

Near the end of August, Muriel and her family moved into their new home in Harford County. One night, if I recall correctly (and one motivation for writing this book is the longer you live, the worse the memory when it comes to details) ... Dena called me and told me Muriel thought about it and had agreed to be my girlfriend and do things together. I was 16 years old; she was 14.

In most relationships of this type, when the infatuation ends, the two go their separate ways. When it starts, you don't even entertain such a thought. I think in this case, I am the one who fell hard for her, and she likely got with me more out of curiosity. It didn't matter to me.

I got the girl. Little did I know this budding bliss and togetherness would set into motion a timetable that moved pretty fast over the next 6 months. One that set the stage for what was to come.

Robert Lawhon, my grandfather, the most godly man I have ever known.

CHAPTER THREE

WORKING DAYS AND HEADY NIGHTS

Late in the month of August of 1974, I was still enjoying my newfound freedom from the routine of attending high school. Having graduated in the 11th grade in May of the year, it felt great not to walk back up the hill to Southwestern High School for another year.

However, mom and dad expected me, because I was still living at home, to get a job, so just before Labor Day I began work as a dishwasher at Rolling Road Golf Club in Catonsville, Maryland. The place was about 3 miles west of my house. Sometimes I took a bus, and sometimes I rode a bike.

I and a few other friends, like Rick Thomas, were encouraged to hire on there by mutual friend Dennis Bell. Dennis had been working there for a while. Rick showed up for his first scheduled day. Four hours into the new job, he was being told what to do by Dennis and then caught heat from head cook Tom Franco, who wanted my buddy to move a little faster in picking up the pace.

Rick's response was to go to lunch. He enjoyed lunch so much, he never went back to work that afternoon. I think they are still waiting for him to show up.

My tenure was a little longer. Because you see, unlike Rick (who was in no hurry to find a girl, to the disappointment of many neighborhood lasses), I had deepened my relationship with Muriel. And buddy, if you haven't got any money to take out the lady, your chances of retaining her tend to decrease rather precipitously.

I rather liked working at Rolling Road Golf Club. In addition to the aforementioned Mr. Franco, you had Miss Mattie, who cooked alongside Tom. A couple of super nice waitresses named Patti and Debbie were also a delight, and let's not forget the young janitor named Bones, who, when he stood sideways, was hard pressed to be seen.

It was also at Rolling Road Golf Club that, unforeseen to me at the time, my desire deepened to begin a career in radio. Here's how that all came to be.

When I commenced my short career at Rolling Road, I took in my beat-up old AM-FM radio, placed it against the window, and then stuck a coat hanger in the hole where the antenna once resided prior to snapping off. I figured music would make the day go faster.

My station of choice was an AM station. 68 WCBM. The station where all the good songs have gone. The Greatest Hits of All Time. I would arrive in the morning, listen to Lee Case wrap up, then Joe Knight would go on the air for a few hours, and he in turn was followed by afternoon drive legend Larry 'Old Dirty Shirt' Walton, to whom I would listen before leaving at 5 every day.

I was never enthralled with washing dishes, but WCBM had a great format mixing oldie with the adult hits of the day, and Mattie and I would sing along. She was a Black lady, very pretty, with a great personality, full of great wisdom and advice. I loved her, and she knew all the Motown stuff WCBM played back in the day. So, we sang together.

I have no idea what has happened to Mattie, but I pray the Lord blesses her richly in all her days.

Tom Franco told me more than once to stop singing and wash the dishes. He was a tough boss but very likeable because he had a great sense of humor. Yes, we had fun.

At the same time when washing dishes, I studied WCBM's format, personalities, contests, and music and was tremendously attracted to and impressed by the whole presentation. Years later, I discovered a fellow named Bruce Holberg was the man who put WCBM's sound together.

Many years later, in the early 2000s, I met and formed a friendship with Mr. Holberg that remains to this day. He left WCBM in 1977 and went on to manage radio stations in Philadelphia.

He then bought some radio stations in Grand Rapids, Michigan, and Wichita Falls, Texas, sold those, and now enjoys his retirement as of this writing.

One day Bruce and I met for lunch at Sansom's Oyster House in Center City Philadelphia. It was a thoroughly enjoyable time. It's not often you get to tell someone who unknowingly, decades before, exerted a tremendous influence how much that meant to you at the time.

I think he appreciated that. I know I sure did. And he paid the bill. If we ever meet again, Bruce, it's my turn to pick up the tab. Thank you.

As Muriel and I spent more time together in the last months of 1974, I began to think about the future. Looking back is 20/20 hindsight, of course, but I made several missteps in my eagerness to plan for the days ahead.

You'll see, as all this is laid out in the chapters ahead, why impatience can really prolong the efforts and distance needed to achieve the goal.

Now at this time in the fall of 1974, I began conversations with recruiters in both the Navy and Air Force. The Army, Marines, and Coast Guard did not particularly interest me, as my mechanical aptitudes or experience were not a fit for either. Furthermore, I wanted a radio career, and not having money for college or the patience to attend, the shortest distance between where I was and where I wanted to go was in either journalism or on-air in the service.

Since I was not particularly interested in serving overseas, I was hoping to train for journalism school out of basic training and get a stateside base to work the military gig and, in my spare time, try to hook on with a small-town radio station around my duty assignment and, for the next 4 years, do both and then separate back to civilian life and devote 100% to broadcasting.

During this time, I had talks with my brother Walt and father to get their opinion. My brother was emphatic that I consider the Navy. He did 4 years there from 1967-71, with most of that time on the Independence in Europe. My dad served on the legendary navy carrier the USS Intrepid during the big war.

I don't recall that Dad recommended one over the other, but all in all I think he was pleased I was going in the service to acquire some badly needed discipline.

Walt's reasoning was that regardless of what I trained for in the Navy, I could always 'strike' or apply for certain types of jobs if I showed a particular talent or interest and there were openings, and I could do this without going through a prolonged process.

Speaking of the Navy, my best buddy Rick enlisted with them and actually shipped out to Great Lakes Naval Training Center in October for what would be a lifelong military hitch of 20 years, followed by the remainder of his work years as a civilian employee at the Coast Guard Yard in Curtis Bay, Maryland.

The Air Force recruiter who eventually signed me, Staff Sergeant Robert Devora, was a charismatic, nice, engaging guy who exuded optimism and confidence. I met him at his office on Frederick Road in Catonsville one rainy day in early November, 1974, to get the ball rolling.

When I shared my interests with him, he said, 'You can guarantee a slot in a particular school like journalism, but you may have to wait in the delayed enlistment programme until it comes open.' Or you can enlist now and tell the career counsellor when you get down there on base that this (broadcasting/journalism) is what you want to do and that you would like to test for it. Take the test, and if they have openings, they will consider you.

Well, it didn't exactly work out that way when I got to Lackland Air Force Base in San Antonio some 90 days later. Even though they had open slots at the time. Eight of them. More on that straight ahead.

Meanwhile, I had to get Mom and Dad to sign off on the enlistment for whichever branch I chose (or would agree to take me). They agreed to do this. Had to pass a security clearance. Pre-medical exam as well.

Later in November, I decided to sign with the Air Force on a standard 4-year active/2-year inactive reserve contract. My reporting induction date was 10 February 1975.

With the decision made, I explained to my girlfriend Muriel that once I had some time in the service, I wanted to make plans to marry her and eventually bring her to the base where I ended up. I shared this with her mother, and she had no objection but preferred that her daughter turn 16 before such an occurrence would sit well with her.

Now given the fact that I was turning 17 and she was still 14 at this time, that all sounded good in theory, but the plan was not realistic, given the fickleness of such a tender age, as I would come to find out. Nevertheless, Muriel said she was on board with those plans, and thus we spent the next few weeks going out, enjoying the holidays, and spending as much time together as we possibly could before I left town.

My sister Lynda and her boyfriend Jimmy would on occasion double date with Muriel and me. We would dine at downtown Baltimore restaurants like the old Emerson's. Muriel was already 5 foot 7, so she was served wine at the table. Being 14 years old, I'm sure she found this a unique experience. I was 6 foot 1, so I too was not deemed to be underage.

Other dates included roller skating, hanging out in the park, and taking walks. The days and weeks went by quickly. 1974 gave way to the brand-new year of 1975.

The weekend before my induction into the Air Force, I spent it with Muriel down in Baltimore. Jimmy and I drove her back home that Sunday night before my departure the very next day. I felt strange and also sad that I was leaving for a long time to come. Earlier that day, my folks had a party for me at the house.

One image I had was of my godly grandfather Robert Lawhon. He loved the Lord and was an inspiration to many. There's a picture of him seated in the kitchen eating cake. I didn't know it then, but it would be the last day I would see him on earth.

After dropping Muriel off and saying my goodbyes, I remember the long drive down US 40 Pulaski Highway into Baltimore. Not much conversation in the car. It was a time for reflection. The only lingering memory I have of that excursion home was Barry White's song 'You're the First, My Last, My Everything' playing on radio station WCAO.

When the song did its long fade out at the end, I immediately realized I was fading out of a lot of people's lives. To this day, the memory remains vivid, like it happened last hour.

I was leaving people who were very special to me, and I was trading it all in for an adventure that went in directions I never thought possible.

Lackland Air Force Base, San Antonio, Texas.

CHAPTER FOUR

WELCOME TO LACKLAND

Monday morning of February 10, 1975, was sunny and cold, and I arrived at the Air Force Induction Center on Elkridge Landing Road. The sprawling building covered a full city block and was just a stone's throw from BWI airport.

Sergeant Devora picked me up at the house on 506 Brunswick Street very early that morning and drove me down to the building.

Induction into the Air Force was a daylong process. Classes here, an exam there, breaks for lunch, and we didn't finish until the afternoon.

The plane departed after sundown for Atlanta, and there I transferred to another plane, which landed at San Antonio airport early that evening.

The aircraft was pretty much a charter flight. All of the passengers were headed to basic training. After landing, we were escorted to a bus that took us to Lackland. When the doors opened, we got our first taste of the rude awakening that was to come.

The T.I. (Technical Instructor), which is the same as a D.I. (Drill Instructor in the Army), was Sergeant Bush. James T. Bush. He sized up the 4 lines of raw recruits standing before him and addressed us as girls, ladies, and rainbows.

The latter term was applied because we were all in different colors of civilian dress.

Most of us were rather stunned and stressed by this sudden turn of events, but some of the recruits were older and weren't at all fazed.

Like a fellow named Earl Hazelwood. I got to know Earl later, and we will bring him into the story at a more crucial time later in the book, but at this juncture he stood in the front line while Bush was walking from one end to the other, reviewing each arrival with a close-up stare that could melt steel.

Now Earl was a Carolina boy, really easygoing, and nothing much fazed him, so when our new overseer stopped in front of Earl and gave him the stare, Hazelwood returned his gaze with a big toothy grin and replied, 'Pleased to meet ya, Sarge.'

That was the first of many times any of us dropped down and did 25. As in pushups. Earl set the pace, as our group, Flight 162, would make its mark in Lackland lore in the 6 weeks that followed. Both for excellence and for notoriety.

As all of this was happening, my grandfather back in Baltimore was preparing for bed that same night and excitedly told his wife about something he found in the Bible. He never got the opportunity to get into details, as the Lord sent the angels to bring him home. In his sleep.

I could write a book on Robert Thomas Lawhon. I was his namesake, and he was the most godly man I have ever known. Born in 1894, he was not yet 81 when he departed. He was playing baseball with the kids in the schoolyard while in his late 70s. Always on the go. Always joyous. A great sense of humor and such energy all the way to the end.

When Grandpop went home, it was without seeing most of his grandchildren come to a saving knowledge of Jesus Christ as Lord and

Savior. Since that time, just about every one of us made that decision to do so.

He planted the seeds by taking us to Sunday School as little kids, and he was always praying for us. Grandpop was known for picking up neighborhood drunks on Sunday morning and, much to the chagrin of my unsuspecting grandmother, piling them in the car and driving them to church to hear the gospel.

Some parents leave a legacy of money, or possessions, or fame. Robert Lawhon left a legacy of Christ. Which in my view is of far more exceeding value.

Sergeant Bush called me in the next day and informed me of my grandfather's passing. 'I just got word from the Red Cross for me to tell you that your grandfather passed, Mathers, up in Baltimore. Normally we allow recruits to leave for this, but the decision was made to not allow you to go home because you have only been here for two days, and it might disrupt your training.'

The more likely explanation was they figured I would not come back if allowed to leave. The first couple of days of basic training were most challenging due to the methods employed in transitioning a civilian to military life.

That Friday was Valentine's Day. Late in the afternoon we were all given an opportunity to make a phone call to someone. I chose to call my girl. However, earlier that morning, I received my first letter from her.

It wasn't exactly a 'Dear John' letter, but it sure felt like one. She said, 'I went skating and met this boy named Ralph Horton. He is nice and wants to take me out...

Oookay. Am I getting the kiss off here after less than a week in San Antonio? It wasn't one my best weeks. Dealing with the sticker shock of military harangue and then hearing about this little development back in Edgewood, Maryland.

The call went okay and she assured me there was nothing to it. Still, it seemed these cryptic messages said otherwise.

What was it the Buffalo Springfield said in that 1967 hit of theirs...

'Paranoia runs deep. Into your mind it will creep'

However, I didn't have time to dwell on this development. There were bigger priorities. Like adjusting to Air Force life. We were in formation before daybreak and going at it with one thing or another until lights out at 2000 hours (8 pm).

The weather in San Antonio in February and March is relatively mild. The nights were somewhat chilly and the days could get warm. Even hot at times. For one thing it was a lot nicer than where I had flown in from.

My Father wrote me a rare letter which I received about 10 days into training. He told me about Grandpop's funeral and the weather in Baltimore, which in his usual colorful manner, he described as 'colder than a welldigger's a--'. He also reminded me that I would be able to adjust to military life. Just hang in there with the training.

That advice came in handy in the days to come in one respect, to which I will elaborate momentarily.

Lackland Air Force Base was in 1975 a sprawling complex of barracks, office buildings, and training fields. From the moment the bus rolled up to the guard booth near Interstate 410 and State Highway 90 to the time a recruit stepped foot off that bus, every minute of your time for those six weeks of training was accounted for. They made it clear right off the bat that you were now their property.

I was placed in a group of recruits called a flight. Flight 162. We were a rather rowdy bunch, and that helped me in no small way to adjust to military life.

My love of music and oldies was shared by other guys in the barracks. One good old boy from the southeastern US named Jimmy Jones was always belting out hits of the day. His favorite was 'The South's Gonna Do It Again' by Charlie Daniels.

Dennis Swartz was from the town of Coventry, Rhode Island. We named him 'Reds' because of his red hair, and he would also belt out a few tunes along with a never-ending series of caustic one-liners, which we all found rather funny.

Each of us received the six-stroke haircut (shave) within a day after arriving. When Swartz saw the damage done to my dome, he promptly tagged me with the nickname of 'Pooh Bear,' in honor of Winnie the Pooh.

Almost everybody acquired a nickname. We were a pretty tight bunch. When not in class or marching or taking physical training, we hung out in the dorm and shared stories.

One day I was chin-wagging at my locker with a fellow recruit named Bob Biermann. It was a very important conversation that, had I listened more carefully to what he was saying, his words would have given me more insight as to what I was up against in achieving my goal of media training.

Bob was a confident, mellow kind of guy who told me he came in to train for a slot in American Forces Radio. He also said he was at one time on the air at some small-town radio station before enlisting. This quickly got my attention, as he both did and was going to do more of the type of work that I joined the Air Force to learn about and start my career.

He surprised me at one point in the conversation when he said his training wasn't going to happen and the Air Force was giving him a choice of either doing something else in the service or getting out altogether.

I reconnected with Bob nearly 50 years later, and he recalled the exact set of circumstances as pertained to him.

'Yes, I was in for a brief time. I left just before the end of basic training when the guaranteed job they promised me vanished. I and a few others were offered money, an honorable discharge, and 6 years in the Inactive Reserve. I got there in January and was on the way home by the end of February.

Biermann continued, 'When the planes changed in Atlanta, I decided to visit my family in South Carolina instead of heading to upstate New York. It was the best decision I could possibly have made. I actually took the Greyhound bus from the old Atlanta airport to Anderson, South Carolina. Within a few days I had a job at WLET AM/FM in Toccoa, Georgia. On that very first day, I met the woman that I would marry just 6 months later.

Biermann also recalled the Air Force at that time in early '75, had to reduce numbers by nearly 20 percent as the Vietnam War was coming to an end (that would happen officially in May).

For some reason, my idealistic and disbelieving 17-year-old brain did not put two and two together at the time. Essentially, what I was facing was no chance of getting what I came in to do. If guys like Biermann, who signed up and received a GUARANTEED slot in American Forces Radio, were having that opportunity shut down after signing on the dotted line, there was no way that they were going to even allow me to test for the opportunity.

About halfway through basic training, I met with a career counselor. After telling him what I was interested in and that I would like to apply for radio or journalism training, the counsellor explained there were 8 openings for journalism training at Fort Benjamin Harrison, Indiana.

Then came the crusher.

'There are others with more time and grade who will likely fill those openings. Like an E-4 member (Sergeant) or one higher in rank. However, we'll let you test on the general curriculum and see where you will best fit in.'

What could I do? No chance of even applying for the slots. They decided after reviewing my test scores that I would best fill the needs of the Air Force as a computer operator or Russian language specialist.

Russian language? I was still trying to master the English language, for crying out loud.

Computers is where I ended up.

Which I figured, 'Heck, computers are something I never thought about. I will have to make the most of the situation because I have no choice. At some point down the line, maybe in a couple of years, I'll find a way to get that journalism or broadcast training.

An encounter with another airman months later would give me a whole different perspective on what happened during that career counselling session. Which we'll cover a couple of chapters later.

Inside and outside view of the dorms where we were housed in 1975.

CHAPTER FIVE

BASIC TRAINING

The days of February 10th through the latter part of March, 1975 were as I remember, days that got better as they went along. The introductory basic pay was $361.20 a month, but the money would not be released until after training and schooling.

That was another factor that figured prominently in what was to come.

We actually had three (3!) T.I.s, or technical instructors. They did the same thing as drill instructors in other branches of the military. That was unusual. Most flights had one throughout. Some had two. We had 3.

Their names were Bush, Brown, and Stevens. Bush retired, Brown replaced him, and Stevens came in somewhere in between as sort of a placeholder.

As noted previously, Bush was a Mississippi boy who was lean, wiry, chiseled, and no-nonsense. You didn't want to get on his bad side. He surprised us all by retiring a couple of weeks into our training. Lee Stevens was a stocky fellow who was somewhat quiet but had a big, bellowing voice.

And then there was Sergeant Brown, who replaced Stevens and took us the rest of the way. He resembled and sounded like Lee Marvin but was a bit more tempered and expected us to act like men yet allowed us to loosen up when the work was done.

He got the word I was a speed reader and had me rattle off a couple of paragraphs in front of the boys. I did okay. They applauded. He smiled.

I've placed a picture in the book showing Lackland. One includes an inside look at the barracks. We were taught how to create and maintain a tight appearance in that place, and then our locker contents and bunk had to pass inspection.

More than once, a guy's drawer was yanked out of the locker and dumped on the floor with instructions given to fix it immediately.

One day, a recruit named Donald McLeod didn't impress Bush with his locker presentation. The airman was told to empty a drawer, take it with him to the shower, and clean it out while singing 'Row, row, row your boat, gently down the stream.' Merrily, merrily, merrily, merrily, life is but a dream.

McLeod had a good singing voice, stayed on key, gave us all a good laugh, and we moved along. I wonder where McLeod is today. I liked that fellow.

As I recall, Bush stayed on for a few days to help his replacement acclimate to the flight. Or learn more about us.

Bush, in front of all of us, told Stevens (who was the temporary T.I. until our eventual leader Brown arrived) that we were a motley crew.

He also told us to get ready for a base commander 'pass and review' parade out at the grounds. This was where all flights in training marched in front of the brass, one after the other, and were rated as to their ability to step lively and precisely.

So we went. And we marched. And Bush came into the barracks later that day after it was over to tell us how we did.

He started to berate us and then broke into the smallest trace of a smile and proceeded to tell us we achieved double zeroes.

A perfect score. Not one mistake according to the judges.

Well, of course, this bunch started to congratulate each other, but Bush quickly chimed in by saying, 'It's nearly 2000 hours. Lights out soon. You've got a lot to do tomorrow. 0500 comes quickly.

And with that he was out the door.

A couple of times during basic, we did kitchen patrol. More commonly referred to as K-P. We rose at 3 in the morning and were marched to the dining hall. After arriving we were assigned individual duties.

One of those times we did breakfast at the WAF (women's) dining hall. I was working back in the dishwashing area and would stand at the window as the girls would bring up their dirty dishes, and they would give them to us before heading out for the day.

I saw an opportunity to brighten things up a bit. We worked with other guys from other flights during K-P, and one of these recruits was a good-looking fella. A real Romeo. So, whenever a pretty girl would come to the window with her tray, I would lean over close and confidential-like to her and say, 'See that guy back on the dishwasher. "He's really sweet on you, and he'd like to get to know you."

She'd look over my shoulder, make eye contact with the guy, and smile. After this happened a few times, he said, 'What's going on?' I explained, 'Those girls dig you, man, and maybe you can line up a couple of dates when we get some liberty.'

He took it all in stride, and we all had a laugh. Then one girl came up, and as I received her dishes, she started chatting with me. And then flirting with me. I took the bait and returned the favor.

We were about 30-40 seconds into our conversation and rather enjoying the back-and-forth discussion when a face appeared out of nowhere.

A female instructor. She told the girl to move along and gave me an icy glare that could freeze the leaves on a Florida palm tree.

Oh well, it was fun while it lasted.

At one point in training (remember the Vietnam War ending was drumming guys out of the military left and right), I was called in and asked if I was a drug user. My response was maybe 3-4 times did I ever take one hit off of a joint, but no, I never used pills. I was a straight beer drinker at that time.

Well, about a week later I was called back in and offered an honorable discharge because of my admitted 'drug use.' I told them no; I wanted to stay in the Air Force, and nothing more was mentioned after that.

Physical training was a big part of basic. Later in the training, our squad leader (the flight was broken down into 4 groups of guys) Each group was a squad. Joe Putnam from Massachusetts was in danger of being set back and not graduating.

We had to run a mile and a half wearing full uniform and boots and finish it in 16 minutes. Joe did so many things right, but this was his Achilles' heel. I think he had breathing problems.

The last Saturday of training, Joe had one more opportunity to prepare for his test on the following Monday. The rest of us had already tested and passed. I did my mile and a half in 12 minutes and 35 seconds with full gear.

I volunteered to go with Joe out to the track, and we ran together. I offered advice on pacing, slowing down and controlling his breathing, getting into a rhythm, and mentally focusing on the goal.

It worked. He passed. I was so happy for him because he was a super nice guy who helped others (including me on a number of things) and was glad to see him make it!

Near the end of basic, we were given some liberty. One such occasion saw us getting on a bus and taken to the Hemisfair Arena to see the great Bob Hope perform. That was neat.

Then on Day 25 of our training, we got full liberty. The whole flight was taken into downtown San Antonio and dropped off for a day of doing whatever we wanted to do. Unchaperoned. Uh-oh. However, the bus would leave San Antonio at 5 pm to come back to the base. We had all better be on it or could be hit with a U-A (unauthorized absence) and punished.

Well, we had a little situation arise where a favorite of mine, James Mroczek, was the oldest recruit in the flight. He was 25 years old. Much more mature, much more worldly, and a bit more independent. He also needed to buy a vowel to complete the spelling of his last name, but we didn't hold that against him.

Mroczek joined the Air Force to land a special skills position as an artist. Very specialized position. My brother Walt was one of only 125 artists in the whole United States Navy back in '69-'70, and he like Mroczek was an independent guy to say the least.

Artists are very creative thinkers and go where the wind takes them.

That day in San Antonio, the wind took Mroczek to many places in town, and when the bus loaded up at 5 PM and drove back to Lackland, old Jimbo wasn't on it.

1975: An Incredible Journey

We had to immediately line up for a head count after getting back to the dorm. Mroczek wasn't there. This required some creative thinking.

At some point, one of the people in authority asked where he was. What followed would have made a great script for an episode of the TV show 'McHale's Navy'.

'Does anyone know where Mroczek is?'

'Sir, I understand he may have gone to sick call, sir!'

A few minutes later, somebody spotted him walking into the dorm. He was all smoked up as my father would say. Plain drunk in any language.

Miraculously, no authority figures were present when Mroczek came in singing and loudly proclaiming how he ran his own life and he decided to come back when he was ready.

Nobody knew just how he got back and made it through the gate without alerting a sharp-eyed guard who could have turned him in. Probably took a cab. Anyway, he ran the gauntlet, and now it was incumbent upon us to try to deliver him to safety.

Immediately, about 3 or 4 of us hustled him to the shower, stripped off his clothes, threw him under a hot stream of water, and left him there for a few minutes.

Then we hustled him back into his clothes, dragged him around the corner to his bunk, threw him in the sack, put the blanket up around his neck, and told him to lay there and not make a sound.

He immediately fell asleep.

A short while later, the instructor comes in and asks, 'What's Mroczek doing in the sack at this time of day?'

Sir! Mroczek feel sick in San Antonio, and was given orders to rest as apparently he was out in the heat and may have developed sun poisoning, sir!!'

Notice we used words like 'may', 'apparently', and so on. One had to cover one's flank and not tell a direct lie. After all, maybe the combination of alcohol and sunshine did adversely affect his well-being.

I went in to the service weighing 192 pounds. I came out weeks later at 164 pounds. My mother saw me next time I got home and wondered what happened.

Actually, I liked Air Force food. It was at Lackland that I tasted yogurt for the first time in my life. I also liked the option of taking whatever I wanted to eat in the buffet line, and boy did I chow down more often than not.

My metabolism was just burning up the calories and the pounds.

Sure wish I had that to work with today.

It was also in dining hall that local top 40 radio station WOAI in San Antonio was played throughout the seating area. That meant a lot to me. You see, Basic Training isolates a man from the world. Those songs kept me connected with my hobby of music and my aspirations of getting into radio.

Just like the days a mere 4 months before when I washed dishes in Catonsville at Rolling Road Golf Course listening to WCBM radio. At that point in time, November 1974 seemed like a lifetime ago. So much had changed.

Lots more changes were in the offing. We finally graduated and received our schooling assignments. There was a little sadness over people going their separate ways, but that was far outweighed by anticipating life at the next station of Air Force life.

I hopped on a bus that took me out of San Antonio on a Thursday morning, up north through Lubbock, and then into Wichita Falls, Texas.

Goodbye, Lackland. Hello, Sheppard.

It was the end of March, 1975. Now in a new place, and time to go back to school.

1975: An Incredible Journey

Group picture of me, my classmates, and instructors from May 1975.

CHAPTER SIX

SHEPPARD DAYS

The first guy I met when arriving at Sheppard Air Force Base in Wichita Falls, Texas was the leader of our new dorm, Darrell O'Neal. Darrell was an Airman First Class who acted like a T.I. welcoming new recruits. He was intent on telling us basic training grads how to live and conduct ourselves when in our apartment and away from school.

He did not have an easy job, to say the least. When you're working with a bunch of fellows who just arrived from basic training and, apart from attending class, now find themselves with lots of time on their hands, the task was akin to corralling a greased pig at the county fair.

I spent a mere 8 weeks at Sheppard. The facility was a technical training center where newly graduated airmen fresh out of basic training were introduced to the schooling they would need for the jobs they were to perform.

Mine, of course, was computer operator. A far cry from pursuing my passion to become a radio announcer or journalist, but at the time I figured this was all that was available to me, so let's do the best we can.

I embraced the training and scored high marks in the 90s, making graduating a done deal. In 1975, the average person never really thought of computers, and the world in general was nearly 20 years away from employing their use in a personal fashion.

My stay at Sheppard got off to a 'flying' start you might say. Before the training even began.

Those of us at Lackland departed San Antonio at daybreak on Thursday, stopped at Lubbock to stretch our legs and grab a bite, and arrived later that afternoon in Wichita Falls. We got off the bus and were given instructions to report the following day for an orientation, then shown to our respective dorm rooms where we would be living for the next 2 months.

The next day we all reported to a large meeting room. A series of instructors and supervisors welcomed us and told us what to expect in the days ahead and what was expected of us.

By 3 o'clock that day, I was getting really impatient for a number of reasons. One was the tedium that had set in. We'd been there most of the day. All of us were bored.

The main reason for my restlessness in particular, was I had hatched a plan (a common thread with me in those days) as to how I would spend the upcoming weekend.

The classes didn't start until Monday. So, I figured I'd grab a ride after the orientation to the Wichita Falls airport, fly to Baltimore, see Muriel and spend the weekend there, and fly back on Sunday night in time to grab a few hours sleep and get to the first day of class.

I scanned the briefing room looking for a friendly face. Specifically, near one of the doors that opened to the outside. The place was packed with over a hundred new arrivals plus the officials.

A sergeant posted at one of the exits seemed awfully approachable. So, I walked up to him and commenced the following conversation.

'Sir, how much longer will we be here for the briefing?'

'Why, do you have somewhere to go? You just got here.'

'Why yes I do. I have to catch a 4:15 flight to Baltimore and I was hoping to get out of here to make it in time to fly up there, spend Saturday and Sunday there, and fly back Sunday night to make the first day of classes on Monday'

'See this door'

'Yes sir'

'I didn't see you leave. Have a nice weekend'.

After receiving that wonderful blessing, I sauntered ever so slowly out the door so as not to attract attention, and then broke into a full run for two blocks back to the dorm, rushed up the steps, grabbed my pre-packed bag, called a cab, then called the airline and asked them to wait until I got there before leaving.

The cab pulled up, I made it with five minutes to spare, and arrived in Baltimore in the early evening.

It was to say the least, a nice 48 hours away. Wonderful seeing mom and dad, and also great to remember how it felt to have your girl in your arms again.

Letters were fine but in no way did they measure up to the real thing.

On my return that Monday, the dorm captain (O'Neal) approached me and wanted to know where I was all weekend. I told him and he replied, 'I rounded up everyone in the dorm to review the orientation and no one could find you.'

When I explained where I was, he in so many words wanted to know if I asked anyone for permission to leave the base period, much less fly out of town. I simply said, 'No told me I had to.'

The classes at Sheppard were actually quite enjoyable. We had several very helpful instructors, and the one I remember most was Staff

Sergeant Hudson. A very personable guy who I also recall frequently using a phrase, 'that's a fact of matter' instead of matter of fact.

We were trained on the Burroughs B-3500 system. A behemoth of a computer. Basics like loading tapes, running card readers, and assorted responsibilities were tied in with it.

My classmates were really super people.

The one who I palled around with the most was a fellow named Bruce Gibson. He was from up around Chicago. One Saturday morning, Gibson and I went to see a local used car dealer. He was interested in buying a set of wheels in the hopes of driving north after school was completed.

When we entered the office at the used car lot, there sat behind the desk a young lad of no more than 15 or 16. A trusting sort. So much so that when he gave the keys to Gibson to test drive a car, he neglected to ask for ID. I was informed of this as we were driving down the street. Gibson said, 'He doesn't even know who I am. I could just take this car and keep it. But I won't.

Smart man.

When we returned the car to the lot, the young man was told 'I'll think about it and maybe get back to you.'

With the afternoon in front of us, we decided to explore north central Texas. We hitched a ride down to a little town called Bowie. We were hoping to get to Dallas, but when no more rides were forthcoming, we decided to have a look around.

We came upon a cattle auction and figured we'd stop in and check it out. There were bleachers where a lot of the locals sat and bid on calves, sheep, and the like. I looked around at all of the spectators. Many of them were wearing Stetson hats. The auctioneer was a fascinating fellow. I couldn't understand him but the natives did, and every time one of them touched the brim of their hat, the price went up.

I looked down at the guy, and at a moment of fatigue, brought up my hand to rub my eyes. Right away, the master of ceremonies pointed at me. I looked at Bruce and he said, 'you just bid on that big steer in the center of the arena.'

Thankfully, someone else quickly 'outbid' me. I froze and did not make a move until the steer was finally auctioned off. I then turned to Bruce and said 'let's get out of here.'

Back out on hot and dusty US Highway 287, we decided to hitch hike back to Wichita Falls. A series of people drove toward us and as they pulled even, would point left or point to the right. This fascinated and irritated me. I thought it was a local custom making fun of hitch hikers.

Finally, a guy stopped and said he'd take us up a little way to the town of Henrietta. On the way, I asked him about the finger-pointing deal and he said, 'that's folks way of tellin' ya they're either gonna turn left or turn right when they get up the road a little way.'

I felt better. A little better.

We were sweatin' up a storm on the shoulder of northbound 287 when a pickup truck pulled over. Hitched to a trailer hauling two steers. We jumped in the back of the pickup, and as we made faces at the steers and roiled them up as best we could, took the ride all the way back to Wichita Falls by late Saturday afternoon.

Gibson never did go back and buy that car.

I got to know others there during my time at Sheppard. I'll start with the classmates, including a blonde lass named Debbie Wherli. She was a pretty girl with the most beautiful legs one could ever imagine in an Air Force uniform. Very smart and conversational, but she was all business, and try as the others might to make conversation with her, she usually fended off the advances with a well-timed one-liner.

We had an E-4 Staff Sergeant student in the class named Lee Robinson. He was a soul brother, personified the word 'cool', and kinda liked it when I nicknamed him 'Lincoln Hayes', after the character on TV's 'Mod Squad'. Which I appreciated because he was as serious as they come. Lee was in his late 30's. He probably felt like a father in some ways to us youngsters. A nice guy who was retraining into a different career field. A 'lifer'. Never knew how he made out but I trust he made out well.

Grady Toland was a fun guy. A Texan through and through, and like many natives of the Lone Star State, tended to tell you that regardless of how impressive anything and everything you, your state, or your experiences in life happened to be, well, his were bigger and better because that's just the way it was in Texas.

Others in the class included guys named Peel, Finster, and Meredith who to varying degrees, were nice, personable folks.

I lived in the dorm with a guy named Tully. We met in basic training and were both assigned to Sheppard. He was from Boston. I was from Baltimore. He loved the pro basketball Celtics and I was a big fan of the Bullets. Golden State played the Bullets in the finals that spring. Tully was disappointed his Celtics lost to my Bullets in 6 games, so he wagered me that my team would lose the championship finals.

He was right. The Bullets went in the tank and were beaten four straight. All close games. It just wasn't the Bullets year.

I was settling in well with the schooling and the course was not particularly hard. Studying with people who became your friends helped an awful lot.

One night I went to the NCO club with another buddy of mine named William Fancher. Not sure why I remember all these folks, but it sure helps when you're writing about a time in your life that happened nearly 50 years ago.

While there, the place was packed with Airmen and WAC's lookin' for friendship and maybe even romance. As the strains of Labelle's 'Lady Marmalade' pounded through the room, I thought of the approaching days when I would be allowed up to a month's leave before going to my first duty station after school.

That leave would of course bring me back to Baltimore and thus to Muriel. She had written to me rather steadily during my time at Sheppard, and began to write her name on the return address as Mrs. Muriel Mathers.

I cherished those letters and whenever I saw an envelope in my mail window, joy filled my heart.

The calls made to her on weekends required lots of change for the pay phone, but I didn't mind. Muriel and I had talked about marriage both before and during my entrance into the air force, which to an outside observer likely seemed rather premature, given that I was 17 and she was only 15. We had known each other for 6 years at that time and figured that was long enough.

Without a doubt, I was living a fantasy that unbeknownst to me at the time would clash with a reality that I would have much rather avoided, but one that was needed and as it turned out, took our relationship in a much different direction. Even more so, one that greatly altered the course of my life.

The Lord says in the Old Testament book of Jeremiah, 'for I know the plans I have for you. They are plans to prosper and not harm you, and to give you hope and a future'.

Much like Jonah the prophet who was determined to go one way, and God directed him to go His way, I would soon be setting a course that was fraught with a lot of danger and risk. At the time I dismissed those hazards, and if not for the Lord's mercies, could have encountered severe penalties from several sources.

We'll get to all of that later in the book at the appropriate time. However, I do think this is a good point to introduce the Lord's Providence and how it affected the events that would quickly unfold.

Before schooling was out, each student was allowed to complete something called a 'dream sheet'. This exercise allowed you to choose up to 7 bases or duty stations where you would be sent after Sheppard to begin your career. Of course, I picked Bolling AFB in DC, Fort Meade in Maryland, and just about every other military post I could think of in the mid-Atlantic area. My thinking was if I could land at one of those, I'd be in close proximity to Baltimore and Muriel. The groundwork would then be laid to start making plans for a marriage.

What I got for a duty assignment never even came close to Baltimore. Not even in the United States.

After receiving my notice of transfer in early May of '75, I looked and saw something that read APO New York. I figured, 'New York is close to Maryland. Yeah, that'll work, or sure. But when reading the fine print, I saw something called 'Tuslog Det 10.' I looked into this further and was stunned to discover that I was being shipped off to the country of Turkey.

That's t-u-r-k-e-y. And we ain't talkin' Thanksgiving with the folks either.

As was my tendency at the time, I ignored the news and focused instead on the exciting prospects of three weeks back in Baltimore. I'd deal with the Turkey 'thing' later.

After graduating the course at Sheppard by the end of May, it was time to say goodbye to the friends of the past couple of months as we all went our separate ways.

Gibson, Finster, and I decided to carpool it to the airport. We set out late in the afternoon in Finster's car and drove down to 287 to Dallas Love Field where each of us would be catching night flights back to our respective hometowns.

One moment of that ride featured a song coming on the car radio.

Dionne Warwick's 'Message to Michael'. I listened to the words while driving through the darkness, and found the storyline somewhat relatable. The girl in the song is missing her man who left town to seek his fortune and promised he'd soon be coming back.

Lyrics included….

'When you find him please, let him know. Rich or poor, I will always love him so'

I was looking forward to seeing the girl that I loved so, and trusted she felt the same way.

Yes, I was really looking forward to getting back to familiar faces and places.

The neighborhood where I grew up. Wilkens Avenue. 1974.

CHAPTER SEVEN

HOME ON LEAVE

I arrived back in Baltimore the last day of May in 1975 and would remain on leave until Monday June 23rd. As I recall Mom and Dad picked me up at Friendship Airport and homeward bound it was to 506 Brunswick Street.

The next three weeks were a blur. Time always flies when you're having fun and I was indeed enjoying myself. Between spending days and nights with family, neighborhood friends, and Muriel…I was busy trying to soak up as much of the home experience before heading back out.

Although I was now officially a trained computer operator with an upgraded skill level, my love of radio was no less passionate. I listened an awful lot to Baltimore radio when I was on leave in June of '75, especially my favorite station WCBM.

The Big 68 playing the greatest hits of all time was like an old friend that I had sorely missed. Back in that time we had no internet and if you didn't live in a certain area there was no way you were able to listen to a station like you can today with 24/7 streaming available anywhere in the world.

WCBM announcers Lee Case, Joe Knight, and Larry Walton really knew how to communicate to the listener. I studied what they did, gave thought to how they did it, and made notes that would help me long into the future.

But the personality that I enjoyed the most on WCBM was Jack Edwards. He was a walking encyclopedia of oldies. Listening to him, I learned so much about the artists and the songs. He was very passionate about the music of the 50's and 60's and also played the current adult contemporary hits of the day.

I grew up with the oldies and never lost my love for them. That dedication would bring me into lifelong friendships years later with legendary disc jockeys like Jack Edwards as well as many of the artists who made the music.

The 24 days at home were a blur, but one funny incident that sticks out (although it was anything but humorous to her) was when I went to Edgewood to pick up Muriel and bring her down to Baltimore for the next day or two. Back then, I did not have a car nor did I wish to inconvenience anyone to give me a lift up and then back.

Edgewood was 30 miles northeast of the city, and a 60-mile roundtrip could use up a lot of gas, priced back then at 55 or 60 cents a gallon. That was not cheap even then, as the energy 'crisis' early the year before had shot the cost up from an early 70's average of 33 cents a gallon.

So, after taking a Greyhound bus up there and spending the day at the house with her and the family, we took one back to Baltimore late in the afternoon. From downtown, we could have waited a little longer to take the number 3 straight to the house, but being very impatient we grabbed the number 11 towards Lansdowne. A route that took us a couple of miles off course but we figured we'd walk it, no big deal.

We got off in front of the iconic Montgomery Ward building at Washington Boulevard and Monroe Street, and thus commenced taking a shortcut and walking the B&O railroad tracks from there up to the neighborhood. About a two-mile walk.

No big deal, unless you are a female who has to take a pee. I felt so bad when about halfway up the tracks, Muriel's knees began to buckle. She could not hold it any longer and was in agony.

It was also pitch-black dark by this time, and we could barely see in front of us. I wasn't concerned about so much about that, considering I hopped freight trains along that stretch many times. However, I had a crisis on my hands. Muriel was one who never complained, and for her to be in such agony told me I had to think of something fast.

What was my next astute move? I handed her several napkins out of my pocket, pointed her to a path leading to the woods, and told her I'd wait and 'stand guard' until she came back. When she returned, she began to admonish me in no uncertain terms that never again did she want me to place her in such a precarious state.

That was nearly 50 years ago. Muriel I would like to for the first time make a public apology to you for putting you through all of that.

The day finally came that I had to say goodbye and move out. Parting was indeed such sweet sorrow but at the same time I was somewhat looking forward to this place called Turkey. I can honestly say I went in to the experience with an open mind. The tour was for 15 months, and September of 1976 would come quickly for my return.

Believing that my training as a computer operator was the only option I had after talking with a career counsellor back in basic training, the prevailing mindset was we would do the best we could in this field and at some point, down the line, look into doing the radio thing.

Mom and Dad along with Muriel drove me to the airport on Monday June 23rd. It was not easy getting on that plane out of Baltimore, believe me. A hug and a kiss and a promise to write were real motivators and the idea was to be optimistic, that it would all work out somehow.

1975: An Incredible Journey

I connected at JFK Airport in New York to Pan Am Flight #1. This was the eastbound around the world flight. After stops in London and Frankfurt, I landed in Istanbul (not Constantinople). Which was a very big city. I had some time to spend before connecting to a flight to the southern part of Turkey, so I walked out of the airport and into the streets to do a little exploring.

I sensed that Istanbul had a very contemporary feel to it. The city was unique in that was influenced by both European and Asian cultures.

After this little sojourn, it was decided to go back to the airport and we headed over to Turkish airlines for the third and final leg of the journey. A flight to the city of Adana.

When I arrived there, the city was somewhat interesting, with its downtown area and every now and then familiar looking city scene. I said to myself maybe this won't be too much of a culture shock after all.

I spoke too soon.

My impression on the way out of town was stunning, but not in a good way. I felt I had been dropped into a place where Lawrence of Arabia was coming out of the hills to skirmish with the Hittites, which made me feel like a Luddite.

As I rode the air force base bus the five or so miles to the base, the sights were something I'd never seen before. People pushing ox carts along the side of the road. Compact European cars speeding along the highway. Barren hills and mountains off in the distance. And lots of desert terrain.

Welcome to Turkey, Airman Mathers.

I could scarce take it in.

.

1975: An Incredible Journey

Incirlik Air Force Base, Adana, Turkey.

CHAPTER EIGHT

TURKISH WAKE UP CALL

After arriving at Incirlik Air Force base on 24 June, I spent the next week in orientation. Both with the new duty station, to the culture of living on base and in understanding the attractions and hazards of traveling off base.

I was assigned to a logistics department near the airstrip. Incirlik was a very important base to the air force and the US military as a whole. Strategically speaking, the base served as central operations for air defense in the Middle East and a deterrent to Russia. Tactical nuclear weapons were also stored there allowing us forces quick response to an attack in that part of the world.

The base opened in the mid-1950's and was used jointly by American and Turkish forces. The facility was also part of the NATO defense system.

In the summer of 1974, Turkey decided to invade the island of Cyprus and captured about a third of the territory. When it was determined months later that equipment issued by Americans were used in the invasion, the United States congress decided to embargo further sales of arms to the country.

The Turkish government responded to this in June of '75 by closing all American bases with two exceptions. Izmir and Incirlik. Both were NATO-designated facilities, and Turkey agreed to allow their continued operation, with the caveat that only NATO activities would be allowed at those installations.

Another result of this development was the stopping of the flow of personnel into Turkey. This 'freeze' was explained to me in my first few days, and apparently, I was in one of the last groups to arrive before the cut-off.

What wonderful timing.

My new boss was Staff Sergeant Roger Barksdale. He was a nice enough guy, very casual, and in some ways reminded me of Ernest Borgnine in the old TV show, McHale's Navy.

His department got the job done, but personnel had no particular interest in adhering to the Air Force dress code. Barksdale would run around with his shirt tail out and an ever-present cigar clenched between his teeth.

Barksdale was respected by the veterans there, but newcomers like me were tolerated at best. I was given tasks to do that really had no bearing on the mission.

I understood this. I was a rookie and really didn't understand what I was to do in the first place. This was my first of two computer departments during my time in Turkey and it didn't take too long for boredom to set in.

I'd show up every day and ask what I could do to help. I was given what seemed like one menial task after another, but what did I know? Maybe what I did was very important. I did what they told me and hoped that it would all make sense at some point.

A few days later came the weekend. This would not be just any weekend, however. I would on that Sunday afternoon unexpectedly encounter a situation that would change the course of my life, let alone my military career.

I set out on a walk to explore the base. My steps took me to a building that housed American Forces Radio and Television, or AFRTS. All at once, I was reminded as to why I enlisted in 'this man's Air Force' to begin with.

With growing curiosity and excitement, I walked up to the door, opened it, and went inside. Looking to my right, there was a fellow sitting in a radio studio. The on-air light was on. He was speaking into the mic.

I didn't make a sound until he turned off the mic. It was at that point he noticed me and beckoned me in to the studio, asking if he could help me.

I introduced myself and told him what I did, that I had just arrived on base to begin my tour, and shared with him my love of radio.

Then, I told him that I wanted to do what he was doing, but was told by the counselor at basic training months before when I asked to test for it, that I had to have either time in service (3 years) or time in grade (e-4, Staff) and I had neither.

Then I noticed as he sat in the chair, on the arm of his light blue, short-sleeved shirt, that he was a one striper (E-2 airman) just like me.

So, I assumed the following….

'I see you're an E-2 just like me. Are you volunteering in this building and if so, who can I talk to about coming here to do the same thing?'

The guy's name was Williams. Rob Williams. He stared at me for a moment and then said, 'what are you talking about? I'm not a volunteer. I trained for this and here I am doing it. My regular duty is announcing and related activities.'

Then he said the words that cut me deep.

Laughing, he said, 'Boy did they pull one over on you!'

He then proceeded to tell me that when he signed up, they tested him for AFRTS and then when he passed, guaranteed him the opening. Turkey was his first duty station out of school. Working as an announcer for AFRTS.

The very thing I wanted to do, but was told was not do-able, was now clearly attainable, but they never gave me the opportunity to at least try.

We chatted a bit longer, I thanked him for his time, and then I left to head back to the barracks.

My head was spinning. I felt very betrayed. The thought of showing up to push punch cards through machines and generate cargo manifests for the next 3 ½ years was something I just did not want to do.

The next day, I went to work and although I did my eight hours, my mind was still trying to process the revelation received the prior day. So, I decided to take my case up the ladder and see about getting a transfer into AFRTS and then grow into the position.

As a 17-year old airman with nearly 5 months of service, I figured it was still early enough in my experience for them to hear me out and move me over.

The stress of dealing with a strange country, doing a job I had no interest in, and discovering an inconvenient truth were a lot to bear.

I decided to place a call back to Muriel the following weekend. She wasn't home. I tried back a short while later, and she was then there. We spoke for an hour. Her mother got on the phone at first and tried to cheer me up as I spilled out my frustrations and loneliness.

She did her best, but when the call ended I was still in the same frame of mind, yet poorer financially. In 1975, international calls were very expensive.

The cost of that hour-long call came to just over $100. That was big money for an airman who at the time was earning about $400 a month. I paid it. In installments.

Meanwhile, it was apparent to SSgt. Barksdale that Airman Mathers wasn't fitting in too well with the crew. More like a sore thumb that was causing him constant pain. The sting of misdirection by the career counselor in basic training was more than sufficient in producing distraction and loss of focus causing me to make frequent mistakes in manifest processing.

Because of my self-consuming isolation, there were few times of engagement with the staff. Yet there were exceptions. One that stands out in mind was a Turkish civilian employee who loved American music.

Tefvik Esberk, whom we called Tommy, was a nice guy and one of the few in the group that I spoke with. One day he shared with me his favorite contemporary song but had difficulty saying the title.

Not because he didn't understand English. He was very proficient in speaking the language. After a few attempts of reciting the title, I figured out what he was getting at, so I finished it for him.

You mean, 'Another Somebody Done Somebody Wrong Song'?

He smiled and said enthusiastically, 'Yes! That's it!'

B.J. Thomas would've loved it.

Within a month of my arrival, I was moved out of Barksdale's boys club and sent up to the base operations computer center.

I arrived there in mid-July of '75. I was introduced to my immediate supervisor. Sergeant Anthony Wells was a California guy who personified the traditional laid-back West Coast attitude. I took a liking to him right away.

I found the environment much more welcoming at the new place.

If only for a short time. The next few weeks would see an unexpected shift in the landscape. Literally and figuratively.

1975: An Incredible Journey

Family members left to right Brother Walt, Sister Lynda, and Me.

CHAPTER NINE

GOING UP THE CHAIN

Over the next few days, I busied myself with getting accustomed to the new department and trying to settle in for the next 15 months.

The assignment in Turkey was an unaccompanied tour. A tour designed to leave the spouse home. Which most guys did, but some figured out a way to circumvent that rule.

My basic training colleague Earl Hazelwood was one such stalwart who figured out what to do. First of all, he didn't want to live on base and who could blame him.

His wife purchased a ticket and flew as a civilian to Adana. The two of them scouted out a nice penthouse apartment overlooking the city and agreed to a long-term lease. Earl then told his boss he was moving off base and would provide his forwarding address.

And there wasn't a doggone thing the Air Force could do about it. I reunited with Earl some 45 years later, and we laughed about that move. Considering what I was soon to do, maybe Earl and Mrs. Earl's initiatives in solving what seemed to be an unsolvable dilemma were rubbing off on me... although my plan would prove to be a lot more perilous.

1975: An Incredible Journey

The barracks were dreary, the atmosphere was uninspiring, and you felt somewhat like you were in prison as life on Incirlik was rather limiting. Be that as it was, I was reeling from the revelation that either my recruitment was handled poorly, or they didn't tell me what I needed to know. It all fell back on me. I had an opportunity to thoroughly investigate what I was getting into but I didn't.

Bottom line was I figured in my particular instance, there was still time as a military member with less than 6 months active duty to plead my case and ask the folks at base personnel to transfer me out of computer operations and into American Forces Radio.

I started by going to my immediate supervisor Sergeant Wells and explaining my dilemma. He was somewhat sympathetic but told me that I really didn't have a chance to succeed and should just try to make the best of it all. However, he assured me I had the right to address the issue and he saw no issue with me taking a shot at asking for the transfer.

My next stop was Captain Gregory C. Clark. He was the commander of my squadron, and he pretty much said the same thing. Take it up the ladder, it was suggested, as he did not have the authority to grant such a move.

Eventually I requested and received an audience with Colonel Nelson, who presided over TUSLOG Detachment 10. I could go no higher on base for such a request.

He listened patiently to my reasoning for wanting a transfer. After I finished my sales pitch with all of the maturity that a 17-year old could muster, he said...

"The Air Force has invested a lot of money and time in schooling you to become a computer operator. The reality of military life is this, Mathers. The needs of the Air Force come first. Now, if you decide near the end of your 4-year hitch that you would like to apply for a transfer, by all means, at that time you can meet with a career counsellor and see if openings exist. If so, that's when you can apply. At that time, you would need to re-up for another four years.

'But for now, the Air Force has determined you can best serve the military in your present skill classification. Therefore, request denied'.

He wasn't quite finished.

'I granted you this meeting because your efforts intrigued me. Let me give you a piece of advice for your young Air Force career. When meeting with a superior officer, you salute upon entry and upon leaving. And one more thing. Shine those shoes. Dismissed'.

Boy, was I deflated. The man told me what I needed to hear, but not what I wanted to hear.

All of a sudden, the dream of broadcasting just seemed so far away.

With slumping shoulders, I trudged back to my room at the barracks. After slumping on the bed and becoming engrossed in my state of depression, I further resigned myself to the inevitable. Turkey for the next 14 months. With no trimmings, so to speak.

Unbeknownst to me, we'd be changing course through an unforeseen development.

One of Martin Luther King Jr.'s more memorable speeches was 'How long? Not long'.

I was lying on the bunk late in the day on that first of August, 1975 asking the same question. The answer came rather quickly.

Before we get to that, as I was lying on the bed having a pity party, in walks my roommate.

Airman Robert Roche was a boy who grew up in the town of Delmar, Maryland on the Delmarva Peninsula. Not far off U-S 50 near the town of Salisbury on the Eastern Shore.

Roche was a very intelligent guy who tended to embrace side hustles designed to make him money. Very smart, somewhat cocky, but just prior to my arriving as his roommate, he escaped a major piece of trouble by mere seconds.

Every military base or post has a Class Six store that sells alcohol to personnel at greatly reduced prices. As you'd imagine this was quite popular among the airmen stateside, and even more so overseas.

Roche decided one day to purchase some very high-grade Scotch and other spirits and offer them for sale at a certain tavern in Adana. In other words, he would buy the booze at low prices, mark it up, and sell it to the locals. He'd give a small percentage to the bartender and still recoup a handsome profit.

He did this a number of times over the course of a month, and one day after walking in with his latest 'bargain' for sale, he went to the well once too often.

Roche would place the bottles on the bar and go sit over in a corner at a table. Some neighborhood guy would come in, bargain a price and make the purchase.

On this particular day, not a potential customer, but two Adana police officers strolled in and walked directly to the bar and commenced conversation with the barkeep.

Danger signs immediately went off in Roche's mind. Thankfully for him, there was a side door out of the place, and he quickly took it.

He encountered more blessings when a cab was waiting outside with the driver inside at the wheel. Roche leapt in the cab, yelled "Incirlik" "Incirlik", and the guy took off.

The drive to the base was around five miles. As the cab was about a mile down the road, Roche turned and looked behind him and saw a police car closing in on him and the cab.

He pulled a couple of large bills from his pocket and screamed to the driver, "This is yours if you get me there before the Polisi (Police) catch up."

As the cab sped up with the cops in hot pursuit, Roche saw the guard gate in sight. About 10 feet shy of the base, the cab screeched on the brake, Roche flipped the money to the driver, bolted out of the vehicle and ran through the gate as the police, who at this time had caught up with the taxi, were preparing to jump out of the car and latch on to the fleeing airman.

Had Roche been caught before arriving on sanctuary soil, he'd have been locked up for sure, and when a U.S. citizen is locked up in Turkey, particularly a military member, there ain't no getting you out.

Two female airmen were doing time in a dirty jail in Adana for selling hash. All the U-S officials could do was visit them and try to cheer them up.

Have you ever read the story or seen the movie 'Midnight Express'? It's the story of Billy Hayes, who was also locked up for drugs in that country before escaping later in 1975.

Check out 'Midnight Express' and you will see that messing with the Turks is not the thing anyone wants to do.

Roche still retained that cockiness following that narrow escape, but he was a lot wiser and to my knowledge, never pursued that kind of thing again.

I told him upon his entering the room what I had encountered by going up the chain about asking for a transfer and he wasn't very encouraging, saying 'sounds like you did what you could. Just make the best of it until you can get back to the states.'

That's what I figured too. Until the next day when I went to the mailbox.

I opened up the door and a brown envelope was sitting in the slot. I thought to myself, 'this looks like the same thing as when a tax refund comes in the mail'.

I pulled it out and yes it was from the U-S Government. Upon opening it, I saw a check addressed to me.

For $526.00.

Attached was an explanation. The remainder of unissued pay from basic training in San Antonio, Texas.

This development unfolded on Saturday. August 2nd. I went back to the room and showed Roche. He thought that was pretty novel. So, did I.

I went to the paymaster on base and cashed the check. I didn't have a checking or savings account so I pocketed the money and kept it in my wallet. Nothing against Roche but no way was I gonna place that wad anywhere except on my carcass.

An idea was growing in my head that weekend. The more I thought about it, the more it appealed to me.

Before the weekend was out, I had made up my mind to go through with the idea.

1975: An Incredible Journey

Entrance to JFK Airport, Brooklyn, New York.

CHAPTER TEN

COME FLY WITH ME

Looking back to that moment at the mailbox, I had no idea a check was coming my way. It did not occur to me that any money was owed to me from basic training. Ask any recruit who goes through the experience of transitioning from civilian to military life, and they'll tell you the only thing that counted was making it through the program.

The money made it easy for me to take a stab at trying to reach my goal of broadcasting some other way. Had that check not arrived, none of what was to follow could have happened.

I went into work that first Sunday night in August. After grabbing some midnight chow, we reported to the overnight shift at the data processing building. That was one of the more enjoyable 8 hours to date since arriving. My mind was full of excitement and there was a lot more spring in my step.

I then went back to the room, grabbed an overnight bag, packed it with a couple of changes of clothes, a shaving kit, my copy of the orders that got me into Turkey just a few weeks before, and a half dozen cigars (I was a cigar smoker). I left all of my military work and dress attire in my locker. Didn't plan to wear it anyway.

I arrived at the airport via taxi and found out the plane had already departed. After talking to the agent at the ticket counter, I said I would be back tomorrow with plenty of time to catch the Turkish airlines flight from Adana to Istanbul.

I then caught a cab back to the base and walked into the barracks with bag in hand. Upon entering, I encountered Roche who casually asked, 'Where you going with that bag?'

For a moment, I hesitated to engage him but then realized Roche was a guy who took chances and would probably if nothing else find my plan rather interesting.

So, I told him, 'You know they're going to know you're gone when you don't show up for duty tomorrow night. They'll come here and ask if I know where you are. What do I tell them?

I replied, 'Tell them the truth. That I decided to take some time off, threw some clothes in a bag, and you haven't seen me since. Don't say anything else. Let them figure it out, because who knows where I'll end up when this is all over'

That night I went in and worked my shift, got off early, and went straight to the airport. This time, I was on time. I dug into my pocket, and bought a one-way ticket. Not to Istanbul.

To New York City.

I had decided to try to make it back to the states with nothing but an expired set of orders transferring me from Sheppard AFB in Wichita Falls, Texas to TUSLOG Detachment 10, Incirlik AFB, Turkey. Dated 23 June 1975.

What were the chances of that working?

I didn't stop to think about that.

I boarded the plane and after take-off, the flight began its northward journey toward Istanbul. While flying over the mountains, the Turkish Airlines craft encountered turbulence and as the plane was rocking and rolling, the thought occurred to me that I may not make it to Istanbul, much less the USA.

The flight finally arrived in Istanbul. It was early afternoon, Tuesday August 5, 1975. As I walked off the plane and headed toward the terminal, it was decided that I would present my military I.D. and use it to validate my connecting flight to New York.

Pan American Airways in those days offered 'around the world' service. You had Pan Am Flight #2 which went eastbound. That is the flight that took me to Turkey in June of '75.

The westbound service was on Pan Am Flight #1. Both flights stopped at each airport just once every 24 hours. Depending on when you got there, you might have to wait a long time in the lounge before the plane arrived the next day.

While purchasing and processing my international ticket at the counter, I struck up a conversation with the Pan Am ticket agent. A nice man who was bi-lingual (spoke both English and Turkish). That aspect would prove crucial to me in short order.

After my ticket was upgraded to board Pan Am Flight #1, I then proceeded to the lounge to wait for the flight. I had to pass through a checkpoint which essentially allowed me to clear customs and leave the country of Turkey.

A couple of soldiers were standing at the entrance. They were there to verify ID and passports. All I had was my expired travel orders that got me into the country.

I presented first my ID, and then my 'orders'. They glanced at them and began talking to me in Turkish. I looked at them, pretended not to notice the stern looks on their faces, placed the paper back in my wallet, smiled and said, 'thank you'. I took one step to go past them...and immediately felt the pressure of a bayonet at my neck.

Instinctively I realized the travel orders didn't satisfy their requirements. Thus, as they continued to chatter at me and motion me away, I quickly stepped back, and walked back to the Pan Am ticket agent to whom I spoke with moments before.

I explained to him that the guards did not want to let me through and could he help?

He came out from behind the counter and with me trailing behind him, walked the few feet to the checkpoint.

He began engaging the guards, who responded excitedly, and they went back and forth for about a minute with what sounded like an argument. Finally, the conversation ended.

The one guard motioned me forward, and the Pan Am agent said to me, 'We have cleared up the misunderstanding. Let him stamp your paperwork'.

After doing so, the soldier grunted and with a gesture, motioned me to walk through the checkpoint and into the lounge. I was now cleared to leave Turkey.

As I settled back in a chair in the waiting area, the clock said 2 PM local time. The plane would not arrive until 10 the next morning and would leave an hour later.

Meaning I'd be hanging out at the Istanbul airport for 21 hours before taking off on good old Pan Am around the world Flight #1.

Later that afternoon my curiosity got the better of me and I walked back through the checkpoint (my travel 'orders' now officially stamped with the approval of the Turkish government) to talk to my agent of deliverance at the Pan Am ticket counter.

I thanked him for his successful intercession and asked him what he said that caused them to clear me through outgoing customs.

He said, 'I told them America and our country are having very tense relations over the Cyprus issue and the last thing we need is an international incident should you harm this man or lock him up. He is obviously a military member of the U-S. Just let him proceed. They agreed grudgingly that I had a point and said that if I said it is okay, then they will allow you to go through. I said it is okay'

I could have hugged that man. Looking back on it, had the Turkish authorities locked me up, both they and my Air Force superiors down in Incirlik could have really put the punishment to me.

For the next 20 or so hours, I read, slept, walked through the airport, and generally hoped that I could make it out of the country before they caught up to me and took me back to Incirlik.

I needn't have worried. As one of my co-workers at the data processing building told me after I returned (fellow named Hansen), 'They never even went looking for you. They knew you had no passport to get out of Turkey and figured either you'd show up at some point or they'd hear you were arrested and in some Turkish jail'.

The events of the day kept me in a high state of alert. Each time I had to exit the waiting room and return again, those Turkish gendarmes viewed me with a combination of disgust and frustration. I dared not look at them.

Whatever that Pan Am ticket agent said to those soldiers that made them clear me for departure through customs sure worked well. It was again another moment of mercy extended by the Hand of the Lord.

Speaking of Pan Am, just after 10 o'clock local time came the announcement over the Istanbul airport loudspeaker that flight 1 around the world had arrived and would soon be ready for boarding.

I must admit that while walking up those steps to enter the aircraft, a huge weight was lifted off my shoulders. In my idealistic teenage mind, I was now thinking more so of getting to Baltimore and beginning my quest to fix my 'problem', and the excitement was building.

As the plane took off and flew into the skies, I made a mental inventory of my possessions. No suitcase, no military clothing. Only civilian clothes. I basically had an overnight bag containing summer outfits, a toiletry kit, and those ever-present cigars. I was on my way.

The plane made stops in Frankfurt, Germany, and at Heathrow Airport in London. The Frankfurt arrival in mid-afternoon stayed over only long enough to let folks off and bring on passengers. Heathrow laid over for a while longer for refueling and crew change, and I was able to go into the airport and look around. It is the only occasion to this day that I have ever stepped foot on European soil. The plane took off in the early evening and commenced its journey across the Atlantic to New York City. It is there that this odyssey really began to unfold.

1975: An Incredible Journey

1975: An Incredible Journey

Clearing Customs at JFK Airport, Brooklyn, New York.

CHAPTER ELEVEN

WELCOME TO NEW YORK

As the view from the big Pan Am jet revealed the shoreline of New York and the plane's descent continued into JFK Airport, I was eagerly and somewhat nervously anticipating my entrance back onto American soil.

I have related to many people over the last 50 years, the event you're about to read, and each time the person hearing it finds it hard to believe. But it did. The key to it all was a series of events that took place between walking off the aircraft and walking out of the airport. An hour of time that would either see me thrown in jail or departing in a cab for midtown Manhattan.

It was an early August evening in New York. I had two checkpoints to negotiate before I would be allowed to leave JFK. The first was lining up to go through customs. This initial point of re-entry was to declare, or produce items purchased from outside the United States and make sure everything (yours truly, especially) passed muster.

I had no exotic animals, contraband of any kind, and I never did drugs, so this phase was rather routine. There was a box of cigars purchased at the duty-free shop at Heathrow that had to be declared.

The first question I was asked was, since I was coming in from Turkey, there were no suitcases or large containers accompanying me.

My answer seemed to satisfy them. That I was here on a short turnaround and saw no need to bring a lot of gear.

That satisfied them at that juncture. Likely because they figured I'd be asked that question again at the next and final stop.

They figured right.

The agent directed me to go over to the next line and clear customs with my passport. Thing was, I had no passport. This was going to be interesting.

So, after ambling up to the table to stand in front of the United States Customs Officer to begin the process of clearing customs, I stood there for a moment and looked over the agent's shoulder. I saw the door open with a taxi driver coming in to grab a departing passenger's bags to take outside and place in the cab. I saw behind him as he opened the door, the streetlights of New York off in the distance twinkling through the twilight.

It was at that point that my resolve hardened. I had to get from here to there. I just didn't know how.

Again, the Lord had mercy on me. Here's how it all went down.

Agent: MAY I HAVE YOUR ID?

Bob: YES, SIR. HERE YOU ARE (I gave him my civilian ID)

Agent: MAY I SEE YOUR PASSPORT?

Bob: I DON'T HAVE ONE SIR (Notice how I maintained a respectful demeanor?)

Agent: WHERE'D YOU FLY IN FROM?

Bob: THE COUNTRY OF TURKEY

Agent: OBVIOUSLY YOU'RE AMERICAN. DO YOU LIVE THERE?

Bob: NO SIR

Agent: DO YOU WORK THERE?

Bob: YES, SIR

Agent: ARE YOU IN THE MILITARY?

Bob: YES, SIR

Agent: LET ME SEE YOUR LEAVE ORDERS

This was it—the moment of 'It's now or never.' Remember, I had no plan as to what I was to say, let alone legal authority to enter the country. So, here's what I did.

I fished in my wallet and pulled out the leave orders that got me out of the country and into Turkey nearly two months ago. I handed the papers to the customs agent.

Agent: WHAT IS THIS? THESE AREN'T VALID PAPERS.

Bob: YES SIR, I KNOW THAT

Agent: WHAT ARE YOU DOING HERE? AND THIS BAG IS THE ONLY LUGGAGE YOU HAVE? WHAT GIVES HERE?

I saw the door open again behind him and saw the lights of New York just steps away. Sometimes the mind can come up with funny things when challenged.

So, I blurted out the following. Ad-libbed. Off the top of my head...

Bob: SIR, I JUST FINISHED WORKING 13 STRAIGHT DAYS OUT ON THE FLIGHT LINE AT INCIRLIK AIR FORCE BASE IN TURKEY. I ALSO HAVE A WIFE AND INFANT

DAUGHTER DOWN IN BALTIMORE. SHE IS DUMB AS A BOX OF ROCKS AND DOESN'T KNOW A THING ABOUT FLYING.

SHE'S ONLY 15. I MARRIED YOUNG. I ASKED MY IMMEDIATE SUPERVISOR TO GIVE ME A 5-DAY T-D-Y, OR TEMPORARY DUTY LEAVE, TO COME HERE, GET DOWN TO BALTIMORE, PICK HER UP ALONG WITH THE KID, AND GET TICKETS FOR THE THREE OF US TO FLY BACK NEXT SUNDAY NIGHT.

THEY DIDN'T HAVE TIME TO UPDATE THESE OLD ORDERS, SO THAT'S WHY I'M USING THEM. I'LL BE GOING BACK ON A MILITARY FLIGHT. IF I DON'T REPORT FOR DUTY ON TUESDAY MORNING IN TURKEY AT 7 IN THE MORNING, IT'S MY BUTT IN A SLING, NOT YOURS.

The agent stared at me for about 30 seconds. I stared back at him. Didn't say a word. This fellow was somewhat confused. He knew there were probably holes in my story that had he taken the time to look into them, would have nailed me.

Maybe he figured I seemed desperate yet harmless, and if nothing else, the story may have been legit, and he didn't either have the time or didn't want to take the time to spend on me any further.

Or maybe he mistook the tension on my face for being an overworked young married man who was missing his woman (he was partly right) and felt sorry for me.

Whatever the reason, next out of his mouth were spoken some of the sweetest words I'd ever heard....

Agent: ALRIGHT, GO ON THROUGH. YOU HAVE A LOT ON YOUR PLATE, YOUNG MAN. I WISH YOU GOOD LUCK AND WOULD ADVISE YOU TO MAKE SURE YOU GET BACK THERE NEXT WEEK.

Bob: OH YES SIR, I CERTAINLY WILL. AND THANK YOU FOR UNDERSTANDING MY PREDICAMENT.

I shook his hand, and as calmly but quickly as possible, grabbed my little travel bag and walked out the door.

When I stepped on to the sidewalk of JFK Airport, I was standing about 6 inches off the ground. I had about $75 left from the original $538 or so that came in the mail a few days before. I spent the first part of that hailing a cab and getting a ride up to Manhattan.

The cabbie dropped me out on 8th avenue and 40th street, not far from Times Square. It was then I realized I made it back home. The night was exciting. Summertime in Manhattan. Walking through the streets. Seeing the signs. Hearing the sounds. I was enjoying it.

All that remained was the last leg of the trip.

I walked into the Greyhound bus terminal and bought a one-day ticket to Baltimore. By now it was around 8:30 PM. I wanted to catch the next bus heading down I-95 and it would not leave until a little after 11. I had a few hours to kill.

I went to a pay phone and invested a little money in a person to person call to 679-6432 (funny how some numbers stay in your mind 50 years later) and asked for Muriel to come to the phone.

As timing would have it, the parents were out and Muriel and her sister were there. She wanted to know where I was calling from. When I said New York City, she told me I was lying and then handed the phone to her sister.

After some back and forth discussion, telling Dena I truly was back in the states, she then handed the phone back to Muriel who then asked, 'What are you going to do?' 'Are you coming here?' 'Why are you here?'

I told her I would let her know later when I got down to Baltimore, and then hung up the phone.

11 PM finally came and I boarded the bus. The Greyhound pulled out from the Port Authority Terminal and drove a short distance through the city streets. Before entering the Lincoln Tunnel to cross under the Hudson and into New Jersey, we encountered a long stop at a traffic light.

The window on the bus was open, and wafting down from a second-floor window over the street was the sound of a radio station blasting out of a speaker.

WABC, with Chuck Leonard, as Frankie Valli takes care of business with 'Swearin' to God' on Musicradio 77 W-A-B-C!'

When I heard that, while taking in familiar signs and looking up at the nighttime New York skyline of skyscrapers...I knew I was back in the good ol' U-S-of-A.

And baby, it felt good!

1975: An Incredible Journey

The stop on the road where the driver let me out in the middle of the night.

My home while AWOL. 1974 Sidnee Drive, Edgewood, Maryland.

CHAPTER TWELVE

WE'RE HERE. NOW WHAT?

The Greyhound bus rolled steadily through the darkness down I-95. As the bus rumbled through the Lincoln Tunnel and over to the New Jersey Turnpike, then crossing the Delaware Memorial Bridge and into Maryland, everyone was dozing in the early overnight hours and the only sound heard was the low hum of the engine.

Sitting in the back of the bus, I was wide awake. Thoughts raced through my head. Where will I sleep tonight? How do I find something to eat? My money is getting low and what are my next steps?

My ticket paid for passage all the way to Baltimore, but I had another plan. Muriel lived in a town called Edgewood and the bus would pass a couple of miles northwest of there.

Thus, as the bus passed the Aberdeen exit on that hot night in 1975, I stood up and walked to the front of the bus. Leaning over to the bus driver, I asked him in a low voice, 'Can you let me off on the side of the highway at the Edgewood exit? That is the next one ahead, about 5 miles further down the road. I have no bags loaded. Just me. Hopefully you can allow me to do a quick exit and you can be on your way'.

He replied, 'Why?'

I said, 'I'm a military guy home for a while, and I want to surprise my girl by walking to her house. She lives about a mile off the highway. It would really help if you would do this for me, as going another 30 miles into Baltimore City would mean I then have to find a way to come back out this way, and it is almost 2 o'clock in the morning already.

The driver stated, 'You mean just pull over, open the door, and let you off? You sure about that? On the shoulder of the road?'

I said, 'Yes sir. I have no luggage down in the storage area. Just my carry-on bag. I will get off in 10 seconds, and you can keep going with no time wasted. I would appreciate it very much.'

As the greyhound bus approached the exit on to Maryland Route 24, the driver slowed down, and stopped under the underpass, opened the door, and said, 'Good luck, buddy. Be careful.'

I said, 'Thank you, sir. I am very thankful. Best to you.'

As the bus roared away down the John F. Kennedy Memorial Highway, I climbed up the side of the underpass and on to dark and unlit Route 24, heading for the neighborhood.

The night was quiet except for the loud chirping of crickets and sounds from the nearby woods. I walked a quarter mile east to a section that was better lighted with businesses and parking areas.

At that juncture, Edgewood Road split off to the right and then curved left and went across Route 7 to Pulaski Highway. Having spent a number of days in Edgewood, I had my bearings and knew the short cuts.

I walked on to Edgewood Road, and a short distance ahead was a railroad trestle that went over the thoroughfare. At that point, I climbed up a grade, on to the B&O railroad tracks, turned right, and walked some more. After crossing a little stream known as Winters Run, I looked left and saw the mobile home community where Muriel lived. By now it's almost 3 o'clock in the morning.

Harford Mobile Village was a new mobile home community, and one of the more modern and scenic of any at that time in the state of Maryland. Muriel lived at 1974 Sidnee Drive. She moved there in 1974, which I thought was a cool 'coincidence'. Her home was on the end of the street adjacent to Chipper Drive, and the park ended just behind her house.

I came off the tracks, shinnied down the hill at Winters Run, and walked toward Sidnee Drive. My intention was to come close to the house and see if Muriel's parents were home, and if not, I would knock on the door.

Her parents some nights stayed out late and didn't get home until 4 in the morning. As I approached the house, I noticed the area behind it was no longer woods, but now under construction. The owners of the community were expanding to build more homes further back toward the railroad tracks and at that time, the property was cleared of trees and brush but not much else was there. Except for a couple of bulldozers sitting in the middle of the site.

I saw Gary May's car in the driveway, so I knew the parents were already home. I then turned around and headed back to the woods near the tracks to hopefully find a place to lay my head and catch a couple of winks before sunrise.

However, I began to hear the rumblings of thunder in the distance. Moments later, the sound got louder, and lightning began to flash in the distance. Then big drops began to fall.

Instinctively I ran to one of the bulldozers, positioned myself under the big canvas tarp draped over it, and laid there as the rain came down in sheets. The wind picked up, lifted the tarp in the air, and I got soaked.

1975: An Incredible Journey

After struggling and succeeding to pull the canvas back down over me and assume the driest position possible, I finally managed in the remaining pre-dawn hours to grab the most exhaustive, uncomfortable, and miserable sleep I could muster.

Ever have one of those moments when you awoke and didn't know where you were? The previous day I was in Istanbul. The day prior, at Incirlik Air Force Base. When I came to on this particular day, the first thing noticed was the sound of running motors. I peeked out from the tarp and saw trucks arriving to the construction site.

I don't recall how many of those workers showing up for the day noticed this wet, disheveled figure crawling out from under the tarp of a caterpillar tractor. I didn't wait around to find out.

When I climbed of off the tractor and placed my feet on the ground, I almost fell. The overnight monsoon had left the ground muddy and wet. I don't know how much work those boys were gonna get done that day, but I knew what my next course of action was.

I walked across the sloppy soup and made my way to the side of Muriel's mobile home. The first thing I did was stand at the side of the bedroom where she and her sister slept, and tapped gently on the window. After a few of those taps, the curtains rustled and Muriel looked out between them with disbelieving eyes.

She motioned to me, go to the side door.

When I got there, both of the girls were standing there at the door shaking their heads and smiling at me. Then another face appeared. That of their mother

The aforementioned Mom Muriel.

We addressed in an earlier chapter our first encounters with her and how to say the least she was not particularly thrilled to see me standing around her daughter.

However, Muriel's mother in that period years later seemed to have a softer, kinder attitude toward me. I'm not sure why that was, but I think Muriel the grandmother may have had a hand in that as I was her paper boy at one time and I always treated her nice.

When Muriel and I became an item in the late summer of 1974 and remained so into the start of my Air Force days, her mother and I got along very well. She told me to respect her daughter, do not do something that will complicate your lives (I knew what she meant by that), and she would appreciate that.

Thus, as I stood at the door of 1974 Sidnee Drive in Edgewood, Maryland that very hot and humid summer morning, I didn't know how I would be received.

I was prepared to move on down the road, figure out somewhere to go, and if I could do nothing more than tell Muriel I was okay and I would come up with a solution. Remember, I had already reached my goal of getting back into the states. The rest of it I made up as I went.

Muriel the mom looked at my pitiful state and said, 'You look like a drowned rat. Where'd you sleep last night? Never mind, come in the house. Do you have clothes in the bag? Here, take one of Gary's bathrobes (her husband), get in the shower, and I'll wash your clothes so you'll have something to put on.

She was my angel in a time of great need.

And I never missed an opportunity whenever I saw her for the rest of her life how much I loved her for doing what she did.

When I came out of the shower, and slipped into some clothes, a nice hot breakfast was waiting for me.

After eating, I proceeded to tell the family this unbelievable tale of how I got from Incirlik, Turkey to Edgewood, Maryland.

They wanted to know what my plans were. I told them I was going down to Baltimore to see a congressman and hopefully he could exercise some pressure on the Air Force allowing me to transfer into American Forces Radio in Turkey.

The first thing I decided to do later that morning was let the folks back in Turkey know that I was no longer around.

I went out for a walk. While sitting on the side of a hill near Frank's Pizza looking down on Pulaski Highway (Frank's is still there after all these years!), I wrote a short note explaining to the Air Force that they need to fix the wrong that was done to me and until they did, I decided to quit the military.

I inserted that letter along with my military ID into an envelope, affixed a stamp, and dropped it in the mailbox...addressed to Commander, TUSLOG DET 10, APO New York.

What did I know as to how they would take that? Not well to say the least. I was just 17 years old and figured they needed to understand I was serious in my pursuit of a broadcasting career, and didn't want 7 ½ more years in this man's Air Force just to get training as an announcer.

Now it was time to get down to business.

For about a week, I made some calls and talked to some people about the best course of action to take. Not surprisingly, folks didn't know how to respond except to say it was a hard position to be in.

Didn't I know it.

1975: An Incredible Journey

Mom Muriel. She became my angel in a time of need. I'll always love her.

CHAPTER THIRTEEN

ALMOST BUT NOT QUITE LIKE OLD TIMES

Late in the afternoon of Wednesday August 6, 1975, the family held a cookout in the driveway of the house. Muriel's family invited their neighbors across the street, the Russells, over to join us.

Immediately I realized that my present status had placed me in an unenviable position. While everyone else on the scene was in a state of normalcy, I was a man on the run. A man without a country. A man without a home. The idealistic appeal of 'standing for what was right' was replaced by the realization that I had to somehow get out of this mess.

During the 10 days or so that I bunked up at Muriel's house, steps were taken to achieve some sort of stability. Like the day she and I found our way down to Mace Avenue in Essex. An area about 10 miles down toward Baltimore, in the eastern part of Baltimore County. We spent several hours walking through the community, searching for help wanted signs. Where I could put in applications for work. My aim was to find a job and start producing income.

Who was I kidding? I got no employment offers, but then the thought occurred to me that even if I had secured a job, where was I going to live? Get a car to drive around? Most importantly, at some point the Air Force was going to catch up with me and I would have to face the music.

No, that was out of the question. Upon further thought, it became evident that I needed to talk to someone in civilian authority who could help me out. I had gone all the way up the chain of command when in Turkey and that didn't work.

That thought further reminded me of a couple of guys in the old West Baltimore neighborhood earlier in the 70's. They were inducted into the service, finished basic training, came home on leave, and decided not to go back.

The image from that time of a helicopter flying over the woods near Gwynns Falls Park and the fugitive soldiers marching out into the clearing and placed into waiting police cars resonated with me.

I didn't want to find myself in that position, although I actually was. The gummint just hadn't caught up to me yet but it would be only a matter of time before they did.

Another memory came to mind. When I was about 12 years old, two official looking men came to our house and knocked on the door. I answered and they said, 'We are looking for Walter Mathers'. I said, 'He's not here. He's in the Navy'.

As far as I knew he was on a ship somewhere in the Mediterranean. However, he pulled a similar stunt as I did. The commander wanted Walt to transfer to another ship and stay on sea duty for the next year.

This did not sit well with my brother as he had had enough of the distant horizons and rolling waves, so he figured the only way to come back stateside was to go on liberty and not return. The crew sailed without him. He stayed out for 30 days, and for the whole time, tracked the movement of his ship, the USS Independence.

When the carrier made port in England, Walt was already there on the dock waiting for them to rejoin the ship. They welcomed him with open arms and threw him in the brig.

Walt did hard duty for a few weeks, but got his wish and never again sailed on a Navy ship.

These men probably figured I was not understanding why they were there. They asked to see an adult. My mother came to the door. They produced ID and requested to search the house to see if Walt was on the premises. Permission was granted. He was not there. The duo asked questions like 'Has he been here? Have you heard from him? If you do, call the number on this card.'

They were looking for him in Baltimore...while he was traveling by train exploring Europe with a fetching blonde lass named Desiree.

That experience stayed with me, and has to this day.

Therefore, a decision was made to start seeking help sooner than later for my situation. My civilian residence was in southwest Baltimore. A fellow named Parren Mitchell was the congressman in my district. I was aware of his anti-war stance and figured he was someone who would be interested in looking into this type of issue involving the military.

I further considered that if I visited his office and found someone to hear my story, that I could get some assistance and maybe the Congressman could use his connections, convincing the Commanders in Turkey to let me move over into radio.

I found my way up to Congressman Mitchell's office on Bloomingdale Road near Poplar Grove Street. It was another hot August afternoon. A friend was kind enough to drive me up there and wait while I had my meeting.

As I got out of the car and made my way into the office, the smell of fresh baked bread hit my nostrils, courtesy of Hauswald's bakery just a few feet away. A familiar scent that would make its way down to my neighborhood at times when the wind blew that way.

A wonderful childhood memory. One that seemed so far away at this juncture of time.

An aide to the congressman met with me and heard my story. After finishing, I expected condemnation or a strong admonishment. Instead, he laughed and asked, 'Is this true?' guess he thought I was some kind of nut. Couldn't blame him.

After assuring him it was real, and I suppose after seeing the exhausted look on my face, he reached into his desk drawer and produced a business card.

'Get in touch with this guy at some point and meet with him. If anyone can help you while you're away from duty (a diplomatic way of saying AWOL), he can. In the meantime, I will relay this case to Congressman Mitchell. He spends a lot of time down at the Capitol in DC. but because he's only 40 miles away, he comes to the office at least once a week.'

'I'll make sure he gets this and we will see what we can do, but you have to go back and serve your term while that's happening.'

I thanked him, and as he handed me the card with a handshake and good luck wishes, I read the card. It said...

Chip Cole

American Friends Service Committee

E. 25th Street

Baltimore, Maryland 21218

I went over to see him later that day. He was a young, hip, 70's liberal, a very nice guy, who embodied the AFSC's mission of justice and peace, a conscientious objector, non-violence type of philosophy based on the Quaker movement.

Chip was ready for me, having obviously been briefed by the congressman's aide on the phone before I got there. My situation apparently was more important to them than I realized.

Like the Congressman, Cole said, 'We will look into this, I can assure you of that. In the meantime, you need to go back on active duty for anything we can do to have any positive effect. What are your plans?'

I replied, 'I'm going back. I don't know the day, but soon, pretty soon. I've been here in town for the better part of a week and already I'm thinking sooner than later. No sense in delaying the inevitable.'

'There's punishment coming, I knew that would be the case when I hopped on the plane to head back over here, but I need to make sure I am doing everything I can to convince them to correct this error in employment'.

I also said I would likely turn myself in to the authorities at Dover Air Force Base in Delaware. Upon hearing that, Mr. Cole gave me another business card.

He said, 'Her name is Linnis Cook. She is an attorney who works with the American Friends Service Committee on special cases. I think your case is pretty special. You need to talk to her, get on the record with your story, and if anything happens in Dover that would be particularly questionable, call her.'

'She lives a little north of Dover and can be there if needed'.

I thanked Chip, and went on my way. Later that day, that call was made and after introducing myself, Linnis and I spoke for a few minutes on the phone. She said she would do whatever she could and to call when I made it back to Dover to let me know how I was doing.

All of this made me feel better.

Not only did I have a plan of action (which is why I came back to the states in the first place), but I had documented activity should the Air Force need proof of my motivation for taking the unauthorized junket back across the pond.

For the remaining days at Muriel's, I tried to spend the days in an enjoyable manner. I went boating on the Chesapeake Bay down at Miller's Island, took in a double feature at the Bengies Drive-in in Middle River, played baseball with the kids around Edgewood, and got in a lot of walking.

One day Muriel's mom sat me down and said, ' I called your mother and told her you had very little clothes or personal items. She'll be up here today to see you'.

When mom arrived, I was overjoyed to see her. The first thing I did was apologize for what I did and told her that dad will not be happy. She replied, 'He doesn't know and I will leave that for you to tell him'.

My father served with distinction on the USS Intrepid in World War Two. The Navy never left him. He gave me the middle name of Halsey, after the commander of the fleet, Admiral William F. 'Bull' Halsey.

A snapshot of the thank you card from Halsey to my father is included in the book. It is well-preserved after 65 years.

Mom stayed a couple of hours and then headed home. She is the nicest, kindest person I have ever met. Her support and encouragement tempered with reality and wisdom were very instrumental in strengthening me through the experience.

Muriel's mother was also supportive. I basically had two mothers during this time.

Toward the end of the week, mom Muriel said, 'I think you need to set a date to go back. I was thinking how about this Sunday? Gary and I will drive you up to Dover. The whole family will go and we'll have steamed crabs and whatever else you want up at Jackie's Bar Harbor Inn on Pulaski Highway'.

I replied, 'Yes, that will work.' So, we agreed to leave around noon on Sunday, go and eat, and then take the 90-minute drive over to Dover Air Force Base.

This conversation was on a Thursday. In the meantime, I was wondering if Muriel and I had a future. She was growing somewhat distant from me with everything that was happening. Looking back years later, it was understandable. The girl was only 15 years old and I was expecting her to be more supportive. Her head was in a different place than mine, and my insecurities of future prospects with her prompted me to do something that was the beginning of the end of the courtship where we were concerned.

Up to that point, she and I were talking marriage and then her coming with me to Turkey. I didn't find out until very recently that her grandmother (who knew her granddaughter quite well) advised Muriel's mother to grant permission for her to marry me, that she can sign since she was underage, and allow her to go overseas.

This was done to make Muriel think about what that meant, and true to form she said, 'No, I think I will stay here and just see how everything works out'. Muriel wants something that she can't have, but then when she is told she can have it, she thinks about it and decides she doesn't want it.

Smart grandmother.

I am a big baseball fan and have always rooted for the Orioles. I wanted to go see the team play before heading back to Turkey. There was a doubleheader scheduled between Baltimore and the Texas Rangers at Memorial Stadium on Friday August 15.

The Birds were in second place and having a decent year. And it was 2 games for the price of one. I figured this was a great opportunity.

I told Muriel that I was going to take her to see the Orioles, buy box seats at field level, and do it up right. She wanted to know where I was getting the money.

The reply was, 'I've been sending you money since basic training. You have the money'. She said, 'I really don't want to blow that money on a night out. You want to do this more than me'.

I strong-willed her and told her to please give me the money. All of it. She did. As I recall, she was holding $115.00. That's like $625.00 in 2023 value. That was even more impressive to a young girl who was still in high school.

Muriel pleaded with me. I won out, but eventually, I lost her. That move served to create anger on her part and deepen mistrust on mine. We were 'still a couple' and would be for a while longer, but not much longer.

She and I took a cab to Memorial Stadium from Edgewood. We sat in the seats and watched each team win one game. We stuffed ourselves on pizza, beer, hot dogs, soda, you name it.

The games were long, nearly 20,000 people in the stands, and after the last out was made around midnight, we then took a cab back to Edgewood.

The money was blown. Muriel was furious. I had also bought her a ring the previous fall. She never wore it again.

The next day was a recovery day, and Sunday we made the trip up Route 40 to Dover.

Putting it in perspective, August of 1975 was a tough time for me. I left my job, became a military fugitive, and for all intents and purposes lost my fiancée. All that...and the month was only halfway over.

I savored the crabs and sides at Jackie's Bar Harbor Inn that Sunday afternoon. The ride to Dover was quiet, and reflective. Only the musings of mom Muriel and chatter of young Paul broke the silence.

As I recall, when the brown Plymouth pulled up to the gate and I told the guard why I was there, my thoughts immediately fast forwarded to Air Force stuff.

After a kiss that felt more like good-bye than see you later, I bid Muriel and family farewell and proceeded through the gate to the next stop on this odyssey.

It was at this point that things got even more interesting.

Patterson Park Pagoda. Baltimore, Maryland. Where a city policeman roused me from sleep and chased me across the park.

CHAPTER FOURTEEN

YES SIR, DOVER AND OUT

As I approached the entrance to Dover Air Force base, I felt almost a sense of relief. Whatever lay ahead for me, at least the running was over.

Or so I thought.

Upon entering the building, I was referred to a staff sergeant who worked the desk for the military police squadron. I don't remember his name, but rather his personality.

I told him who I was, why I was there, and told him I wanted to get a military flight out of Dover and head back to Turkey with the intent of rejoining my command.

This short, stocky fellow had a sense of humor when he said, 'I don't know anything about this. Your name isn't coming up on the wanted list'.

I assured him this was all on the up and up.

He sat there, thought about it for a moment and then said, 'Well you're not my problem and I have other things to deal with. There is a plane going out of here tonight. Walk on over to the base airstrip, go into the office and tell them who you are, and they'll get you on'.

After our 10-minute conversation, he probably thought the challenge was solved. What we both soon discovered is that this part of the episode was only beginning.

I strolled across the base. It was about a 15-minute walk from security ops to the aviation building. Dover is a very big base.

After I stepped inside, the guy behind the counter came to engage me. He was the only soul in sight on that Sunday afternoon. Upon hearing my request for a plane ride, he said, 'Sorry buddy. We don't have anything going that way until tomorrow night. Do you have any papers authorizing space on the flight?'

I answered, 'No. The Sarge just told me to come over and hop on the plane'.

The guy smiled and shook his head. 'Sorry. Come back tomorrow'.

After leaving the conversation and going back out into the sunshine, it occurred to me that I had time to kill for 24 hours. It also dawned upon me that the Sergeant really didn't want me around.

I decided to head down to Baltimore. Not Edgewood. I'd already said my farewells to Muriel and the family.

Moments later I was standing out on US 113 with my thumb out to head north toward Baltimore.

About 10 minutes later, this sporty red convertible pulls over on the side of the road and the driver was a very pretty brunette with long hair, sunglasses, and lovely legs. She asked where I was going.

When I told her Baltimore, she said, 'Me too. Hop on in'.

The conversation was nice, the scenery was attractive, and the warmth of the sun was such that I began asking myself if I really wanted to head back to turkey.

Any delusions of changing my direction were dashed when she let me out on Pulaski Highway in east Baltimore. Now I had to figure out what my next step was. I found my way down to the Inner Harbor and called my friend Billy Thomas. He was understandably surprised to hear from me and agreed to meet up with me.

He met me along the wall on President Street where the Jones Falls emptied into the harbor. We shook hands and I told him all about my experience. He found the tale incredible to believe, but since we had known each other a long time, it made sense to him.

Billy is the brother of the aforementioned Ricky Thomas. We all grew up together in southwest Baltimore. During our teenage years in the 70's, we did things like hop trains, walk the streets all night, and pull pranks when boredom set in.

Let me digress for a moment and recall one such occurrence that took place when the owner of Dan's Sub Shop became of interest to our mischievous ways.

Dan Brennan was a kind and laid-back man. He was a tough character too. Dan was the victim of several robbery attempts. Once he was stabbed and suffered life-threatening injuries. Another time, the perp held a gun to his head, pulled the trigger, and the gun misfired.

Mister Brennan was loved by many in the old neighborhood. As I said, he was a gentle man, except when his Irish temper got the best of him. Then, look out.

One guy in the neighborhood was John Brooks. He was a body builder and could handle himself quite well with anyone who gave him a hard time. Until one day when he got on Dan's bad side. Dan flew out of the sub shop, chased John down the street and after collaring him, only eased up when John pleaded desperately, 'Don't hurt me Mr. Dan, please don't hurt me Mr. Dan'.

This particular summer day in 1974, after being up all night walking the streets, I got the idea at daybreak to head to a phone booth and call three cab companies at 10-minute intervals. In each of those conversations, I asked each dispatcher to send a cab to Dan's Sub Shop at 401 Millington Lane. I asked each one to make sure the cab arrived later that night at 6 o'clock.

That wasn't all.

A call was made to the Parker Bus Company asking that a 40-seat charter be delivered to Dan's Sub Shop that night at 6:15, as we were taking a bunch of staff and friends to see the Orioles play that night at Memorial Stadium.

A final call was made to Attman's Delicatessen on Lombard Street requesting a party tray for 40 to arrive at 6:15 as well for this imaginary outing. That didn't work, because I was laughing so hard they hung up on me.

Good thing that happened. Because the other calls found their mark.

We all went home to sleep and woke up sometime in the afternoon. I called the Thomas boys after I hadn't heard from them and reminded them that in one hour, those cabs were coming to Dan's.

My phone call woke them up out of an afternoon siesta, but they knew they couldn't miss this spectacle, and thus I saw them about 15 minutes later running up Dulany Street from Westside Shopping Center to meet me on Millington Lane.

We walked down a half block and stood in front of the Holy Cross churchyard. At 6 o'clock on the dot, there they came. All 3 cabs at the same time. Diamond, Checker, and Sun. The front of Dan's looked like a cab stand at Penn Station.

The drivers got out, went in to Dan's, and about 5 minutes later walked out laughing and got in their cars to drive away.

The bus? You guessed it. It too arrived on time. The driver got out and walked into the sub shop.

We waited a little longer before we saw him emerge. The driver was walking backward. With Dan walking forward. Pointing a finger at him and in no uncertain terms telling him to clear out.

Many years later, Billy did side jobs for Dan on fix-up projects as the old boy owned a bunch of rental homes. Billy dropped subtle hints on one occasion asking him about the time somebody called cabs on him. Apparently, Dan never found out who pulled the prank, because he laughed and said, 'Probably some local kids who had nothing better to do.'

Sitting there on the harbor wall that day in 1975, I told Billy I felt like the guy in the Edward Everett Hale book, 'Man Without a Country', adding 'Isn't it interesting how I'm 2 miles from my house and I can't go home? I don't have a home anymore. Not until this gets straightened out.'

As the day wound down, Billy had to get on home. And I had to find somewhere to sleep. I thought about it, and figured the best thing for me to do was stay off the street until I got back to dover on Monday.

I traipsed east along Eastern Avenue for about a mile until I reached Patterson Park. By this time, darkness had set in and I was tired. In front of me was the famous Patterson Park Pagoda. I walked up to it and saw a little area where I could throw my bag of belongings down and stretch out to get some sorely needed sleep.

It was not to be.

I drifted off to sleep only to be awakened a short time later by a light shining in my eyes. I should have played it cool, but I jumped up and begin to run through the park.

I heard a voice, 'Stop! Police!'. That scared me even more and I accelerated my slim carcass into overdrive and left him behind.

However, the officer had a 2-way radio. The great equalizer. I ran the better part of a mile to the other side of the park, and as I approached the swings at the playground at Linwood Street, 2 Baltimore City police cars swarmed to the spot with engines roaring and lights flashing. They cut off my exit.

I calmly stopped and waited for them to get out of the car and come to me.

'Why are you running?'

'I was laying up at the pagoda and somebody shined a light in my eyes'.

'Did he identify himself as an officer?'

'Not until after I started running. You can't trust people out on the street these days'

'What's your name?'

At this point, my brain went into fast thinking mode. If I give them my name, they might lock me up in City Jail, and I wanted no part of that. Remembering the conversation with my friend just a short time before, I responded...

'My name is William J. Thomas.'

'Where do you live?'

'2135 McHenry Street'

'Why were you laying up there instead of going home?'

'It's been a long day. Out walking, it's Sunday, the busses don't run as frequently so I wanted to get some rest and then head home'

1975: An Incredible Journey

The one officer bought my story, the other one didn't.

He said, 'you have no ID on you'.

'I lost my driver's license when I fell in the water going fishing last week and I am waiting for a replacement ID'

Is there anyone who can back up what you're telling us?'

'Yes, my brother Tommy'

'Is he home now?'

'I think he is'

'What's the phone number?'

'3-6-2-2-1-4-4'

The officer got on the police radio and had his dispatcher patch in to make the phone call. From what I could pick up, Tommy indeed answered. Hallelujah!

I knew Tom well enough to know he was no friend of law enforcement in those days and would give them as little information as he needed to.

'Do you have a brother named Billy Thomas?'

'Yeah'

'Is your address 2135 McHenry Street?'

'Yeah'

'Is your brother born August of 1953?'

'Yeah'

'Okay thank you, sir'

As the officer disconnected the call, it occurred to me he never asked Tommy to describe his brother. Had he done that, I'd have had to explain the discrepancy.

This was the 70's. My hair was military cut. Billy had hair down to the small of his back.

The officers said, 'Go on home Mr. Thomas, and in the future when a cop says stop, you stop. Is that clear?'.

'Yes sir. I'm sorry and I won't let it happen again'.

After the cops got in their cars and left the park, I sat on a bench and contemplated my quandary.

I somehow managed to find somewhere to hole up out of sight and grabbed whatever sleep I could.

The next morning, I fished a card out of my wallet and called a number collect. The number of Linnis Cook. The lawyer who lived in Delaware.

We chatted for a few moments. I told her about my trip to Dover the previous day and how I came back to Baltimore when they couldn't fly me out on Sunday.

She wanted to know if I could catch a bus to Dover. I told I could and she asked me to call her back with a time and she would meet me when I went back to dover air force base.

I called Trailways down on Fayette Street and they had a bus going to Clemente's Travel Center at Route 40 and 13 in Delaware. I called Linnis back and told her what time the bus would arrive.

She said, 'I will pick you up at Clemente's and drive you down to Dover'.

This was certainly an unexpected blessing. I was going to have legal representation. She met me at the bus station and when we arrived at Dover Air Force Base, the ensuing discussion was most interesting.

First of all, when we walked into the base police station, there was the same guy who met me the previous day. As best I recall, the conversation went along these lines.

Sarge: 'Oh, you again. You didn't get on that plane. Where've you been since yesterday?'

Me: 'They had no planes for me to catch so I hitchhiked down to Baltimore and now I am back here to try to work something out'

Sarge: 'Yeah, we'll work something out alright. I'm gonna lock you up and hold you until we get paperwork back on you from your duty station in Turkey'

Then, Mrs. Linnis Cook stepped in and said, 'Sergeant, you can't lock him up'.

Sarge: 'Why not? He's Air Force property and we'll take it from here'.

Linnis: 'Where is his military ID?'

Sarge: 'Why do you ask that?'

Linnis: 'Sir, I know military regs, and if you have no absolute proof of his identity, you could be making you and the Air Force liable for false imprisonment of a civilian. Regardless of what he tells you, until you verify who he is, you're leaving yourself wide open for trouble'.

Sarge thought about that for a moment, and then said....

'Well, we will verify that at some point'

Linnis said, 'Fine and until you do I will assume responsibility for him. Here's my number. When you hear back from whomever you have to hear back from, call me and I will direct him to report to you'.

Then, Linnis added a little zinger over her shoulder as we walked out the door.

'Next time Sergeant, I would suggest you do your follow through and make sure you can deliver on your promises so as not to inconvenience my client who came here in good faith for your help and you somewhat blew him off'

His reply? 'Good day, ma'am. We will be in touch'.

1975: An Incredible Journey

Dover Air Force Base, Dover, Delaware.

CHAPTER FIFTEEN

LIFE WITH LINNIS AND ON THE MOVE

Although I knew the efforts of Mrs. Linnis Cook had secured me but a temporary reprieve, it nevertheless put my mind at ease. I now had time to think. Even more importantly, I had a place to sleep and food to eat. At least for a day or two.

One day at dinner, she served me a bowl of soup. Yogurt soup. Ice cold yogurt soup. Mrs. Cook and her husband were into ultra-healthy eating. I was a fast food, meat and potatoes kind of guy.

Nevertheless, I was appreciative of everything and most thankful for these new experiences.

I spent time with her and her husband for the next 5 days. Walking, having a conversation, and receiving a much-needed recharging of physical and mental batteries. They had a place under the Route 13 bridge that spanned the Chesapeake and Delaware Canal. Lovely people indeed.

It would be needed for what lay ahead.

Eventually the call came from Ol' Sarge down at Dover.

A copy of the military ID card I'd mailed back to the base in Turkey on August 6th was sent to Dover, and that notification made it official that they had their man.

Linnis drove me back to Dover to again voluntarily surrender back into military control.

It was the morning of August 25, 1975.

After Linnis left the base, the Sarge and I spoke a bit. He asked, 'Whatever possessed you to do what you did? If they decided to arrest you at the airport, you could be in a Turkish jail with no hope of ever getting out'.

I told him, 'I feel so strongly about training into broadcasting with American Forces Radio, and considering the fact that I was not told the truth down at Lackland, I figured this move on my part would let somebody know I was serious'.

After our conversation, I went to the chow hall to grab some lunch and then when returning to the police station, Sarge gave me the news that they couldn't get me out on a military hop that night.

It would have to be the next night...and they had nowhere to bunk me up for the night. He could have put me in a jail cell, but he figured since I had already turned myself in twice in the last week, yours truly was no flight risk.

I was told, 'We don't care where you go, just be back here in my office at 1300 hours (1 pm) tomorrow. I have orders to put you on that plane. If you're late, you're in trouble'.

Where could I go?

To Baltimore, of course.

Since I was at this time returned to military control and technically no longer AWOL, it was decided to go home to 506 Brunswick Street and wait for Dad to get off of work.

I had a key to the house and arrived there about 30 minutes before he came home.

I was standing in the kitchen leaning up against the stove when I heard someone coming in through the front door. It was dad.

'Hello Dad'. He looked at me like he wasn't quite comprehending what he was seeing. After a moment, came the inevitable question.

'What are doing you home, boy?'

I then asked him to grab a seat and proceeded to tell him the whole story, concluding with an apology if I let him down and disappointed him.

He paused for a moment and said, 'The military isn't the way it used to be. I can understand why you did what you did, and it was good that you turned yourself in, but you know you're gonna have to face the music when you get back there'.

I told him I was aware of that but that it was important to me to come see him and explain what was going on before I headed back up to Dover to grab a flight back to Turkey. I owed him that. I respected his love and dedication of military service to do otherwise.

My next step was to go to my sister Lynda's house and get some sleep. Early the following morning I took the number 8 bus downtown to the Trailways bus station.

The schedule had me arriving in Dover just before 1 PM.

I switched buses at Clemente's Travel Center at US 13 and US 40 and headed south toward Dover. I was exhausted and promptly fell asleep on the bus.

The bus stopped at Dover. On time. I didn't get off.

I was sleeping and did not wake up until arriving at a little terminal at Seaford, Delaware.

Ironically, I would be living in Seaford less than two years later while working at my very first radio station doing the all-night show.

The bus driver roused me out of my exhaustion to let me know that he was at the end of the line and I had to get off. When discovering I'd overshot my stop by 40 miles, I asked him what time it was. He replied, 'about 20 after 1'.

That woke me up to the reality that I was already late, and likely in trouble.

All I could do was explain my predicament and ask for a return courtesy fare to dover, and somewhat to my surprise the ticket agent inside the little shack agreed to put me on the next northbound bus.

Obviously, she felt sorry for me. I arrived at Dover AFB around 3:30 that afternoon, and when I walked into the military police post, there was our 'friend,' Mr. Staff Sergeant.

And unlike the Trailways ticket agent in Seaford, he didn't feel sorry for me.

After informing me that I was 2 1/2 hours late, a fact that I shared with him was also known to me, he made a phone call and said, 'Come down here and bring so-and-so with you.' I have a duty for you. Won't take long.

Two security policemen showed up and Sarge, while pointing to me, said to them, 'Take him and lock him up'.

I protested, 'Now wait a minute sir. It wasn't my fault I was overcome with exhaustion and overshot my stop'.

Sarge replied, 'It's gonna take awhile for us to get you out of here and return you back to your squadron in Turkey. Until we make those arrangements, you're staying with us. Don't worry (as he smiled), we'll feed you and although our beds aren't the most comfortable, they sure are better than those on the bus.'

'Get him out of here!'

The jail cell had ceilings about 10 feet high, with bars that went all the way up as well. The cell was about an 8 x 10 enclosure, very clean, well lit, with a toilet and a hard bunk. I began to experience a little claustrophobia after a few minutes, as I had never been locked up in my life. However, I said to myself, 'Could be worse. Could be in Baltimore city jail. At least here you'll be fed halfway decent chow, and not get beaten up by others.'

Upon further reflection, it occurred to me this fellow wanted me out of here as soon as possible, so I was hoping my stay would be short.

My stay was that of 2 days.

On Thursday, August 28th at 9 am, the guard unlocked the cell and escorted me back to see the Sarge. I began to think this guy lived here. Then again, he was probably starting to feel the same way about me.

He wasted no words.

'Mathers, I have been informed that regs for whatever reason, probably because the Turks are not on good terms with us, will not allow someone in shall we say, your classification, which is an exclusive one at that time, to return back to Turkey on a military plane.

They say you gotta go back on a commercial flight.

Which means I'm turning you lose. Again. For the 4th time. Here is a travel itinerary and a couple of items that will get you back to your duty station.

First, here is a one-way bus ticket to the Port Authority terminal in midtown Manhattan. When you get there, take this additional voucher and go to the Carey Transportation window. Tell them you want a ride from 42nd Street down to JFK airport.

Here is still another voucher for a one-way ticket to Istanbul with a connecting flight to Adana, Turkey. When you arrive at Adana, there will be two military patrol members waiting to escort you back to Incirlik Air Force Base.

Ol' Sarge then concluded with the following...

'We are not escorting you to New York. You will go there on your own. Largely because I think since you keep turning up like a bad penny, you're not the flight risk you would normally appear to be.

At present you are not AWOL and have not been since you turned yourself in a week and a half ago. But...if you do not make it to New York and or get on that plane, we will not wait 30 days to come for you.

We'll be on your trail. We will find you. And we will throw the book at you. You'll be classified as a deserter and will most certainly receive a dishonorable discharge along with a lengthy punishment.

Do I make myself clear?'.

My father couldn't have made it any clearer, and he was a man whom I feared.

I replied, 'Yes sir. If I run into any issues I will let you know'.

Sarge stated, 'There won't be any'. Then motioning to the two guards still in the room, he said, 'Take him down to the bus station and sit there until he gets on that bus and leaves the terminal'.

Sarge was firm. But Sarge was wrong. He would soon see it wasn't the easiest thing to keep a bad penny from turning up.

As the bus headed up US 13 heading for the Delaware Memorial Bridge, I looked out the window and wondered what could possibly go wrong?

The answer to that question would come pretty quickly.

The Port Authority Building, Midtown Manhattan, New York City.

CHAPTER SIXTEEN

THE SIDEWALKS OF NEW YORK

The Trailways bus chugged along through the hot and steamy day up the New Jersey Turnpike. It was early afternoon when we reached the tunnel that took us under the Hudson River and into Manhattan.

After stepping off the bus, I entered the big terminal and asked someone at the information booth how to get to the Carey Transportation offices to exchange my government approved voucher for a ride down to JFK airport.

Having gotten directions, I calmly strolled in, introduced myself, and presented the voucher, stating, 'I am a member of the United States Air Force and was told to show you this piece of paper so I can get a ride in one of your taxis from here down to JFK airport.

The guy looks at the voucher, then looks at me and says, 'I have no idea what to do with this'. I replied, 'I just told you'.

He said, 'What I am saying is we don't honor anything from the government. We have never to my knowledge transported anyone unless they pay cash'.

I asked, 'How much from here to there?'.

He says, 'About 20-25 dollars and that doesn't include the tip'

I said to myself, 'Here we go again.'

After explaining to the agent, I had no money, I thanked him for his time.

As I walked out on to the crowded sidewalks of a mid-afternoon in New York City, the words of the Sarge back at Dover began to ring in my ear about staying on the yellow brick road.

I walked down the street and honestly had no idea of what to do, or where to go. I went block after block heading south down what was either 5th avenue or Broadway, one of those streets. I then saw something that caught my eye.

A sign over a doorway that said 'Salvation Army Headquarters'.

Here's what I did next. I found a phone booth across the street from the Salvation Army building and called the Sarge.

Collect.

I had his name and direct extension on the travel orders.

He answered and after I introduced myself, he said, 'Oh no. Come on, man, what is the problem this time?'

My response was, 'Well it is a problem. Carey Transportation won't honor the voucher. So, I am marooned in Manhattan, just walking the streets trying to figure out what to do. I'm calling you to let you know. What do you want me to do?'.

He said, 'Turn yourself in to the nearest military base or office, there has to be one around there somewhere'.

I said, 'Well...there's a salvation army headquarters right in front of me. I will get off the phone and go there and turn myself in and they'll work something out, maybe they'll call you and come up with an idea'.

The next thing I heard was a loud laugh on the other end of the phone, followed by muffled conversation. Sarge must have not known whether to laugh or cry considering I remained his problem until I got back overseas.

'Go to the nearest police precinct and tell them what the problem is. They can probably do something. Get back to me when you figure it out. That's all I can tell you'.

With that pearl of wisdom, he hung up.

Now that I had contacted the Sergeant at Dover from a phone booth in New York, I had to get resourceful. As much as I was somewhat enjoying the adventure, I knew I had to get out of Dodge and go back to Turkey. This production was starting to wear on my nerves.

It was unforeseeably one of the most logistically challenging goals I would ever accomplish in my young life.

My next step was to cross the street and walk into the Salvation Army building. The nice folks were happy to talk to me and I shared my story which they found somewhat fascinating.

My memories of the Salvation Army were that of helping servicemen with free toiletries and a New Testament. They were the good guys and I felt safe with them.

They advised me to go to police station up the street and tell the desk officer on duty about my predicament to see what they could do.

Within a half hour, I stepped into the police precinct. It was an old building. It was a cool old building. Felt like I was walking on to the set of Barney Miller. I expected Hal Linden to come around the corner any moment, or maybe Lieutenant Kojak sending Bobby Crocker down to book me on one charge or another.

The officer on the desk sat there with a big grin on his face as I shared my story. To place it in perspective, the US military wasn't particularly popular at that time in history, what with Vietnam finally ending and the anti-war sentiment still running somewhat strongly against the government.

It seemed like almost everybody I talked to found my plight amusing. Like I was in some way sticking it to the man. I didn't feel that way. What I felt like I wanted to do is sleep for a week. In any event they were most friendly and sympathetic.

Made me feel downright patriotic and joyous to live in the land of the free and the home of the brave. Except I wasn't exactly free and didn't feel all that brave.

A couple of cops walk in and they hang around hearing my story. Finally, one cop suggested I take the subway from midtown down to JFK.

I told him the only problem with that move is the Pan Am around the world flight leaves in the afternoon, and only every 24 hours. There was no way I would make the plane in time on that particular day.

I asked the cops, are there any military bases down near JFK and after looking into it, they determined Fort Hamilton was the closest one.

Fort Hamilton was an army base for reservists situated down around the Verrazano Narrows bridge at the edge of Brooklyn. It was very close to JFK Airport. 20 miles away in fact.

The friendly policeman at the midtown precinct telephoned Fort Hamilton, explained to them who and what he was dealing with. He then said they could get me on a subway out of Manhattan and send me down there if someone could meet me at the Bay Ridge stop near the base.

I will never forget the experience of riding the New York City subway. From inserting the token to looking at the strange lineup of characters milling around, I felt like I blended right in.

In a funny kind of way, what may have seemed eccentric to others was quite normal to me. It was America on a normal day and that was something I missed when serving in Turkey prior to my departure.

Looking back 50 years later on this experience, I could have like thousands of others who were stationed at Incirlik simply went along with the program, served my time, and likely gone back to the states in September of 1976 to serve at a base in the US.

On the other hand, I would never have entered the broadcast field when I did.

I have told many through the years, that the Lord had his hand on me and steered me safely through a lot of unwise if not dangerous decisions made during this period of my life.

My 'decision-making' wasn't done yet as I would learn after arriving at Fort Hamilton on that Thursday night in late August of '75.

Toll booth at the New Jersey Turnpike.

CHAPTER SEVENTEEN

A CAMEO AT FORT HAMILTON

I was given instructions as to who and where to meet the MP's (military police) assigned to meet me when I got off the subway at Bay Ridge. The two soldiers decked out sharply in uniforms (with weapons at the hip) escorted me in an unmarked military car to Fort Hamilton.

As the vehicle went through the entry gate, I was impressed by the panoramic scenery of the big Verrazano Bridge over the Narrows. A big body of water connecting lower New York Bay with the Atlantic Ocean. Fever.' the same bridge featured prominently in the movie 'Saturday Night Fever'. That would come along a couple of years later.

The old fort had been in existence for 150 years at that time. Named for Alexander Hamilton and overseen by Robert E. Lee in the years before the Civil War, the place had a good bit of history. Needless to say, I was making some personal history during my time there, history that was not quite as glorious as that credited to those other fellows.

I was taken into the security building and brought face to face with the desk sergeant. He was a charismatic black fellow whose name I don't recall for sure, but 'Lloyd' comes to mind. This fellow immediately impressed me as someone who could have played the lead role in Shaft. Not a mean guy, but no-nonsense for sure.

He was confident, like one who had the run of the base. Obviously having been briefed on my situation, Sergeant 'Lloyd' said immediately after I was presented to him, 'I've been here all day. My wife is waiting for me to come home. I do not have the time or the patience to deal with this now. Take Airman Mathers to the guest dorm, give him sleeping arrangements and put him up for the night. I want him back here tomorrow at 0700 hours.'

The Sarge had no idea how much I enjoyed bunking up at his base. After sleeping for the last week at various times on surfaces such as concrete, grass, and a jail cell slab at Dover, that bed felt good. Real good. I went in, stowed my meager belongings next to the rack, rolled into the upper berth, and from sheer exhaustion went immediately to sleep. The last thing I saw was the fading twilight coming through the window.

The next thing I saw (and heard) was one of the MP's rousing me out of the sack, telling me to get a move on. After a quick shower, I got myself together and was brought back to security to appear before our Sergeant friend.

On this sultry Friday morning in Brooklyn, New York he inquired about my well-being, and I told him I slept like a baby. He then got to the point.

'We cannot get you out of here until tomorrow night. I cannot keep you here until then, because I prefer that you not hang around and cause a distraction. Since you are considered under military control, you are free to do whatever you want to do and go wherever you want to go but you must report back here by 1530 hours (3:30) tomorrow afternoon.'

Any other person in my situation with no money, no wheels, and nowhere to stay locally would have protested and begged for some accommodations to wait it out. I was not like any other person. To me, for some reason I decided I would go back to Baltimore and see a couple of folks. After all, I was just handed an additional 36 hours of

1975: An Incredible Journey

freedom and didn't know of anywhere else to go but back home. So, to speak.

In case you may be asking, the answer is no. I did not even think of going back to Edgewood to see Muriel. My instincts told me that door was closed and I didn't want to bother her and her family anyway since it was now evident to me that I was becoming a problem to anyone who hosted me for any length of time.

I told Sarge that Baltimore was where I planned to go and asked for a ride to the New Jersey Turnpike (across the Verrazano Bridge and through Staten Island, which would allow me to get to the toll booth and hitch a ride). Incredibly (maybe because he felt sorry for me, and also because he wanted to see if I would show up the next afternoon), he called in two MPs and ordered them to drive me over there. The ride was pretty direct. We pulled out of the base onto I-287 and headed west until reaching the Turnpike.

The guys chatted with me in the car going over and seemed to be fascinated with my story as the word had gotten around about me and my exploits. Such as they were. I told them how I arrived at this point and they both agreed the journey I decided to undertake is one that they themselves would never have tried, but they both admired the reason why I did what I did.

Be that as it may, the MP's dropped me off at the exit, which today is known as the Perth Amboy turnoff, or exit 10. I walked over to this long line of toll booths where vehicles paid to enter the turnpike. I was heading south. Toward Baltimore.

When reaching a spot where I could hopefully coax a ride, I met up with a beautiful young blond girl who showed up at the same time I did and she too was looking for a lift. She was going in the same direction as me. I have long forgotten her name, so in this instance let's call her Amy. Which it may have been because I seem to recall it started with an 'A'.

If this dear lady comes across this book and recognizes herself in the story I am about to tell, it would be appreciated if she could email me at the address provided in the last chapter of this book. For reasons of sheer curiosity, I hope she has made out well all these years.

It just so happened Amy was heading to Baltimore as well, but a different part of the city. That didn't matter to me. I was happy to have someone to talk to. For those of you younger readers, hitchhiking was a very common practice back in the 70's. There was little fear of danger back then, which is why pretty girls like Amy felt comfortable.

We hit it off quite well and were standing there for about 15-20 minutes when we heard a horn blowing. We turned our heads to look in the direction of the blast and saw a guy driving an 18-wheeler semi. He was waiting in line to go through the toll booth.

The man motioned us over, asked where we were going. We told him and he said, 'I'm heading that way. Hop on in'.

I helped Amy up into the truck and then got in next to her. The trucker's name (again, recalling as best I can) was Eddie. We thanked Ed for picking us up and were soon through the toll plaza and tooling down the turnpike.

Ed said he had to drop off a load of freight at a stop in Philadelphia. We said that was fine with us. We were just happy to have a ride. The conversation was pleasant and positive. Eddie's truck was a sleeper cab. The truck was somewhat pioneering for the 70's, featuring was a large area behind the seats where this guy would rest up for the night when driving long distances over several days.

The cab had a curtain pulled across the entrance so we couldn't see in there. The tractor was a two-seater, and Amy sat on my lap for the ride over to Philadelphia, about 80 miles from where Eddie picked us up outside of New York.

We finally reached our destination just after noon. A distribution center for Acme Supermarkets. Amy and I got out to stretch our legs while Ed went back to drop off his cargo manifest to the warehouse guy.

A short time later, Ed walked over to us and asked if he could have a word with me off to the side. I walked over to an area where Amy could not hear the conversation. Ed turned to me and said something like this...

'She sure is a good-looking girl.' I agreed with him. Then he laid this on me...

'I need a favor. Let me coax her up into the sleeper and have a little time with her while we're here waiting for the truck to be unloaded. I would appreciate that and anyway, I'm doing you guys a favor by taking you down the road.'

I then understood what he was asking and told him directly that he was free to talk to the girl and make that proposal, but she may not appreciate that. I then said if he tried to force himself on her and she objected, I would have to step in and do whatever I could to help her.

He then walked away and went over to the girl. After about 30 seconds, he then turned and walked back to the warehouse. A short time later, with most of the cargo unloaded, Ed motioned for us to get back into the truck.

After pulling back onto the highway and driving for about 15 minutes, I sensed a bit of tension in the truck. Ed then said, 'We'll be coming up to I-95 in Delaware in a few minutes. I have to make another stop and I will have to let you out. Sorry, I can't take you down to where you are going.'

Amy and I exited the truck, thanked Ed for the ride, and watched him pull back into traffic and head off down the road.

While waiting to hitch another ride, she told me that when we were back at the warehouse, Ed tried to put the move on her and she at first wasn't sure what to do, thinking he'll leave me here and who knows if I'll get a ride to Baltimore before it gets dark.

She obviously told him no. I explained to her about the conversation I had with him. Amy broke into a big smile and thanked me for being her protector. I liked this girl, yet she wasn't my girl. What she did was her business, but if she was gonna be forced into doing something she didn't want to do, I felt responsible to step in and help her.

We finally got into Baltimore around 6 that evening. The last time I saw her was at the downtown corner of Lombard and Pratt streets. Standing in front of the Civic Center, she was waiting for a bus to take her to Towson and for me it was the number 3 to Wilkens Avenue and Pulaski Street.

Her bus came first. I reached out to shake her hand. She gave me a light hug, a kiss on the cheek, and said thanks. Then my bus arrived and off I went.

I decided that I would stay at my sister Lynda's house for the night and then head back to New York in the morning. I rolled up the steps and into the house just before it got dark. My sister wasn't home, and to be as discrete as possible, I went out on the sunporch at the back of the house, dropped an old blanket on the floor, and went down for the night.

Lynda came home hours later and roused me up, wanting to know why I was there and what I was going to do. My sister was the oldest of 4 in the family. The shortest of 4. And the meanest of 4. One did not trifle with Lynda.

After patiently explaining to her the lay of the land, she said okay and wished me well. I told her I would let her know later how I made out and to be assured everything would work out.

I didn't want to be late for my 3:30 appointment at Fort Hamilton. Last time I did that I spent a day or two in a cell at Dover. The memory was still fresh in my mind.

The next day, Saturday August 30th, saw me rouse up around 8 in the morning. After taking two buses to get me over to Route 40 Pulaski Highway on Baltimore's east side, I began hitchhiking. Thankfully, I didn't have to wait too long.

A big Cadillac Eldorado convertible slowed up and the driver asked me where I was going. I told him New York and he said, 'I'm heading that way'. The black gentleman driver was mellow and very conversational. We tooled up the road as Barry White was playing on the 8-track, and he found my story interesting.

The guy took me into Jersey on the Turnpike and eventually dropped me off at one of the rest stops. That man was a blessing to me. Looking back, I believe the Lord sent him my way. In fact, let me go into this a little more.

When I walked out of the front door at 312 South Pulaski Street in Southwest Baltimore, it was almost 8:30 in the morning when I walked to the bus stop. Recall, I needed to be present at Fort Hamilton in Brooklyn, New York in just 7 hours.

I had no money to catch a bus, no one to drive me there directly, and the prospect of hitching rides to get me across parts of four states to arrive on time was a longshot at best.

The Lord shepherded me all the way. I could recount other stories not having to do with this one. Like the time a year later when one summer night I decided to drive from Baltimore to Norfolk, Virginia to visit my friend Rick at his naval base. I started out at 11 pm. Very drunk. And still drinking. My old 1965 Plymouth Fury was tooling down the Baltimore-Washington Parkway when a cop pulled me over.

After it was determined that I was extremely inebriated, and with more than a half dozen empty Miller High Life 7-ounce pony bottles rolling around on the floor confirming this (it's amazing how we remember some of these little details many years later), the officer told me to go down to the next exit, pull over, and sleep it off!

I decided to drive back to Baltimore. About 30 miles to the north. To this day, I do not remember how I got home. All I remember was waking up the next day in my bed with the car safely parked in front of the house.

I'll maintain to my last breath it was God himself who brought me home safely. Chevy Chase in one of the "Vacation" movies had a station wagon that drove itself to the hotel while they were all sleeping.

I had something better than a self-driving car. Angels sent by the Lord. And this was not a movie, but real life. Oh, for the mercies of the Heavenly Father.

After the man in the Caddy dropped me off, how I got to Fort Hamilton was also a blur. I don't recall the 'travel itinerary' after that. Who picked me up. How many rides I had. Nothing. All I recall was walking into the security building on post at Fort Hamilton and looking up at the clock on the wall.

I'll never forget the time. 3:37 pm. A mere 7 minutes late past the 1500 hours deadline.

My man Sergeant 'Lloyd' looked up at me as I stood before him. He wanted to know if I went to Baltimore. I told him yes, and explained in detail everything that happened. He sat there, studied my countenance, and said 'You know I believe you. Nobody could make this up, let alone a 17-year-old kid. Okay, as far as I'm concerned, you made it.'

It was explained to me that in about two hours, I would be taken up to JFK Airport to catch the plane back to Istanbul. They allowed me to go to the chow hall, where I ate about 2 or 3 plates of food. Growing boy, you know. That and the fact that I hadn't eaten much of anything in days.

Following the meal, I returned to the security building to count down the remaining time until it was time to go to JFK. The weather was overcast that afternoon, with showers and thunderstorms. I seem to remember watching the US Open tennis matches in nearby Queens, hearing the announcers talk about possible suspension due to the weather, and wondering if this would affect the departure of my plane later that evening.

I needn't have worried. The sky cleared, and sometime around 6 pm the MP's placed me in a car and drove me the 20 or so miles up the Belt Parkway to the airport. Emotionally I was somewhat relieved to get back to Turkey and see if my efforts would bear any kind of fruit.

As I settled in to my seat on the big 707 to ride Pan Am's 8 PM around the world flight to Istanbul, my mind began to recap the events of the past 4 weeks. A period which seemed to be a lot longer.

As the plane rose into the fading twilight for its eastbound journey, I nodded off to sleep. It would soon be time to 'face the music'. In a detached sort of way, I was focused more on the continuing experiences of this adventure rather than the real threat to my present and future prospects that lie ahead.

A street in downtown Adana, Turkey.

CHAPTER EIGHTEEN

BACK IN TURKEY

The big Turkish Airlines jet taxied to a stop at Adana Airport. As I departed the plane, walked down the steps, and into the terminal, I was met at the entrance by a couple of Military Police from the base. They said they were there to escort me back to Incirlik. I kiddingly told them, 'Fellas I'm not going anywhere except with you. I've had plenty of time away with my whirlwind excursion halfway around the world.'

My attempt at humor masked the apprehension I was feeling inside. Thankfully the military records which documented the remainder of my military career from this point forwarded have allowed me some sort of factual recall of this period.

The authorities on base wasted no time in administering my case. The paperwork was ready and all complete when I arrived. September 3rd was a Wednesday, and I was summoned to meet with officials regarding my unauthorized absence.

My case was most unusual in a number of aspects.

I clearly went AWOL, but left not only the immediate area, I left the country. With no passport or valid leave orders. While they had to weigh that development in passing sentence on me, the legal folks had to decide how many days to dock me for being absent.

My last duty day before departure to the States was August 5. I turned myself in to the authorities at Dover AFB in Delaware on August 17 (the official date on record). I remained free until August 30 when I got back to Fort Hamilton which in turn ended my 'freedom to move about the country' until I flew back to Turkey.

Then to further compound the problem for them, I kept coming back to military authorities during my experiences. That meant I could be not considered a flight risk nor a violent offender.

Obviously, a lot of thought went into how they were going to punish me. Here's how they handled it.

Captain Gregory Clark was my Section Commander. He would prove to be the most pivotal figure of them all in determining not only my punishment, but my final status at the end of my military tenure.

Captain Clark was a compassionate and understanding man, but he also had a tough side to him as well. If he believed you were sincere, he would help you in every way he could.

On this occasion, he got right down to business.

I met with him in his office and after lecturing me on the folly of my deed, he served me with intent to impose non-judicial punishment. Here is the official charge.

'You (Mathers) did, on or about 6 August 1975, without authority, absent yourself from your organization, to wit: TUSLOG Detachment 10, located at APO New York 09289, and did so remain absent until on or about August 1975.'

Free legal counsel was offered (which I accepted).

Two days later on 5 September of '75, I accepted in writing the punishment with no desire to make an oral or written statement.

The USAF imposed an Article 15 judgment against me which resulted in a forfeiture of $80 in base pay. The verdict also rendered a reduction in rank from Airman to Airman Basic BUT the reduction was suspended until 1 March 1976.

Essentially, they were saying 'we think you are worth salvaging based on your reasons for doing what you did and your actions while you were away, so we're going to suspend the punishment for now but if you mess up again, we'll enact the sentence'.

Now $80 may not seem like much but considering my monthly pay at the time was $402.60, that was a 20% fine over a 30-day period.

In any event, we took care of the matter rather quickly. Now it was time to return to work at the Computer Center where I last reported one month before. It was not certain how the co-workers would receive me but that was the least of my concerns. Nothing at all against any of them. My wavelength was different from the one they were on. My priority lay in somehow getting into broadcasting.

As my integration back into life at Incirlik got underway, it was determined that counseling be provided in an attempt to help me through my issues. This action was clearly to me at the time, my opportunity to convince the powers that be at Incirlik that I could be of help in serving as a broadcaster for the AFRTS station there.

The counselor decided that pursuit of this vocation was something that bordered on an obsession with me. He then contacted a fellow named Ennis. He was the Chief Master Sergeant overseeing my department. Ennis was told to meet with me and figure out a solution to my dissatisfaction.

We met in his office and it wasn't a social call. Ennis exhibited from the start a strong dislike of me to say the least. He couldn't be blamed. He was a lifer who respected and valued 'This Man's Air Force' and I was perhaps viewed as a young irresponsible punk kid who made a fool out of the military and got away with it.

Unexpectedly, largely because I was humble yet determined and paid him respect when he barked questions at me, Ennis began to take me seriously after about a half hour of discussion.

Ennis finally shared with me that if it were up to him, we would not be having this conversation. However, after deciding that I was serious about the broadcasting thing, he made my day by telling me arrangements were made with all relevant parties to allow me to go over to AFRTS on my own time (outside of regular working hours) and be a volunteer.

This news was shocking. Absolutely stunning. I did not obtain the requested transfer but was however granted an opportunity to work at the station.

That's all I ever wanted. A chance. A foot in the door. Something to work with. Had they offered this back in June after I arrived, there is no question I would have never taken the drastic measures that brought me to this point in life.

Ennis told me to report over to the AFRTS building and meet with Sergeant Bernie Indianer. Bernie was a New Yorker. I took to him right away and he liked my passion as well. He laid out the ground rules. 'You are given this very unique chance because of what you went through to get it. But all that means is you have to prove yourself. You're raw. Green. Follow our instructions, do what we tell you, and you'll help us and learn a lot.

For the rest of the year, I was very much enjoying the time as a volunteer with American Forces Radio and Television Service (AFRTS). The supervisors didn't allow me on camera or on the air, but instead employed me behind the scenes in the control room. I didn't mind it at all. I was gaining a lot of knowledge and it was all very exciting to me. Naturally my 'day job' as a computer operator was a placeholder until I could head over to the AFRTS building and go to work.

1975: An Incredible Journey

Duties included switching out reels, running the audio controls during newscasts, filing tapes and other materials, and after some time, actually running the broadcasts of movies, shows, and sporting events.

To the veteran AFRTS staff, I was considered a bit of an oddball. My overseas escapades made their way around the station, and whether or not particular members were irritated by my presence, with the exception of one individual who shall remain nameless and did express indignation when I messed up his on-camera newscasts, never let on. They were kind, and I learned a few things about their professionalism that helped me in later years.

I was considered a fifth wheel, not really important to the mission, and at times I was tolerated. I remained oblivious to much of that because to me, it was not a matter of 'volunteering'. It was to me, the start of my broadcast career. It was taken very seriously. At least for the first couple of months.

Incirlik was considered a secondary outpost of AFRTS. Meaning, we didn't have the capability of showing major events as they occurred, or 'live'. The way it was done back in the pre-technological stone age era of the 70's was as follows.

Rhein-Main AFB in Frankfurt, Germany was the European hub of Air Force TV communications. Say the Baltimore Colts and Miami Dolphins played on a Sunday afternoon. The game would be broadcast live by satellite from America and picked up for televising 'live' to military viewers in Germany. At the same time, the game was recorded.

Following the conclusion of the broadcast, technicians at Rhein-Main would transfer the videotape recording to 16 mm film reels. When that process was complete, the films would then be shipped to the secondary AFRTS stations.

The reels would arrive in Incirlik, scheduled for viewing a few days later, and then that Colts-Dolphins game (or whatever the program was) now in our possession would be televised for the viewers on base.

The turnaround time from 'live' to 'rebroadcast' was on average about 5 to 7 days.

Thus, personnel at Incirlik were used to regular tape delay of every major telecast. It was better than no broadcast at all.

As the days went by, life in Turkey became a little more tolerable thanks to the opportunity for learning broadcasting.

I was not deemed polished enough to actually go on the radio and do a program, but the experience in assisting with TV production with whatever and wherever they could plug me in more than made up for it.

At the same time, I received permission to hang out in the production studio when not in use. It was there where recorded commercials and announcements were put together. This gave me time to work with carts. These were cartridges that resembled 8-track tapes, but were assembled in different degrees of length.

A cart could be 40 seconds, 70 seconds, 2 ½ minutes, or even longer. The continuous loop ½ inch tape ran cross the pads inside the cart which ensured the tape would move across the play heads. Much like a cassette player or reel to reel recorder.

A piece of spliced material would stop the cart when it reached the end of its full time (40 seconds, etc.). When you pushed the play button in the machine, the cart would play again with the same material that was recorded originally.

Carts could be bulk erased and then new material re-recorded.

All of this is probably more than you ever wanted to know about cartridges, but as you can see, this stuff was of intense interest to me and simply confirmed to others and verified to me that this is was all I ever wanted to do.

1975: An Incredible Journey

A picture of me taken in Edgewood, Maryland.

CHAPTER NINETEEN

A BREAK IN THE ACTION

The days went by quickly as October wound its way through the Fall of 1975. My volunteer hours at the American Forces Radio and TV station at Incirlik were at some points more than the regular shift spent working overnights at the Computer Center.

A typical 24-hour period for me around this time was reporting to AFRTS around 3:30 and assuming controls at the board to run audio and load reels for the evening news. Sergeants Gary Gilbert and Joe Sargent were the anchors and I studied their delivery, countenance, and enunciation as they delivered the events of the day.

These little nuances would stay with me and help me when I got into the business later on.

Then one day a letter appeared from my buddy Rick Thomas. My childhood friend was at this time serving his first hitch in the Navy. Rick obviously loved variety. He would do anchors aweigh for 4 years, then enlisted in the Air Force at the end of the 70's, and after that, moved over to the Coast Guard in the early 80's. Military life agreed with Rick and he went on to 20 in uniform and another 20 as a civilian Coastie.

The boy did alright for himself.

In his letter, Rick displayed a rather creative cartoon of his pal being chased by a Turk brandishing a scimitar with the intent of poking a hole in my carcass.

What got my attention however was the news he was heading back to Baltimore in late October to go on leave for a couple of weeks and asked me to put in as well with my superiors for permission to join him.

This was exciting news. Rick and I in those days were known to bring lots of long green to the local watering holes on any given day, as between us well over a dozen frosty mugs were extinguished as engaging conversation ensued and laughter reigned.

In the naivete' of a 17-year old, this seemed like a sensible idea. After all, I came back to Turkey on my own, had established myself as a responsible employee at two different duty stations, and figured this would be a nice reward for the lad in exchange for all of this.

But...it was not to be.

My meeting with both the Chief of Data Automation (Captain David Knitt) and his NCO Assistant (Master Sergeant Clyde Rivette) was short and curt. Both men could not believe the gall and hubris created from even asking them to consider such a request.

Obviously, they had not forgotten the events of a mere two months ago. I tried to convince them to look at the present, and the future, and consider how well I was doing after such a difficult situation. No dice.

After sending Rick a return letter telling him he would have to do the tour of our favorite Westside refreshment landmarks without me (including those most enjoyable frosted mugs at Vandy's), I then resumed work but with just a little less zeal than before.

So much so, that my immature response to being turned down was to go out and tie one on. After reaching a state of drunkenness, it was then decided to walk over to AFRTS and report for my volunteer hours. I wasn't even there for one hour. The NCO took one look at me and ordered me out of the building.

This did not place me in good stead with certain people at the radio-TV operation. In fact, someone later shared with me that my indiscretion was expected due to my past performance and some were hoping I would be barred for good.

However, there were supporters who were rooting for me, most of all NCO Bernie Indianer. I liked that guy. He was a New Yorker. Blunt and candid, yet understanding. He told me it was most important not to let this happen again or I'd be gone.

For a while, I kept my nose clean (as Dad used to say). The drinking had to go and for a time it did. A few weeks went by and we straightened up our act.

In November, my Squadron Commander Clark was also trying to help me. One gesture he made was to invite me to attend services at his Mormon meetings on Sunday.

As I recall, I went to at least one and possibly two gatherings. My mindset was so intent on crawling out of my emotional misery that I prayed for the Lord to give me understanding and even accept the Mormon belief. The Mormons are some of the nicest people you would ever meet.

Today as a born-again follower of Christ, I have had over the better part of 50 years many experiences with other churches and Christian employers. Many times, when either working for or attending institutions stating a representation of the Lord, the human frailties emerged that at times did not give a very positive testimony of Christ and His ways.

Conflict would emerge and division would result.

The Mormons on the other hand, never exhibited any of this kind of behavior. However, the harder I tried to embrace their faith, I did not experience a peace or an interest in wanting to know more about what exactly they believed. At one of those meetings at Incirlik, I placed my head down and prayed for God to show me that this was the way.

It never happened.

What I came to learn years later, is that the Mormon faith acknowledges Jesus as the Son of God, but denies His Deity as God the Son. I pray for my Mormon friends that Christ will reveal Himself in the way He truly is.

One day in late November of '75, Captain Clark and I had a conversation about where I was both mentally and emotionally at the time. He complimented me on my performance at the Computer Center and encouraged me with the AFRTS volunteer experience. He said in essence that in spite of my periodic filings and irresponsibility, I was making progress.

He then asked me if I would like to have permission to take an official leave the following month and go back to the States for Christmas.

You wanna talk about happy? It didn't take me long to respond in the affirmative.

That meeting left me with much joy and a lot of questions.

I wanted to see Mom and Dad. See my friends. I was being given an opportunity to actually go home and stay with family as opposed to my AWOL experience when I was 'A Man Without a Country'.

And then there was Muriel. My girlfriend. From the time I arrived back in Turkey and over the next three months, I had received maybe one letter from her in all that time. That didn't bother me, because my mind told me that things were still okay and just getting with her again would smooth over any problems or misunderstandings and we would pick up with our relationship and tighten things up between us.

1975: An Incredible Journey

As December of 1975 rolled around, I was happy for another reason. The Baltimore Colts were having a storybook year. The team traded legendary quarterback Johnny Unitas after the 1972 season and the next two were losers.

1975 was supposed to be another bad year and things sure started out that year when the Colts lost 4 of their first 5 games. However, new blood like Bert Jones, Roger Carr, Glenn Doughty, and a much-improved defense started winning.

And winning. And winning.

The day of December 14, 1975 was a day (and night) I remember well. The Colts were in Baltimore that day to host the Miami Dolphins. Don Shula coached the Colts for most of the 1960's, but when Baltimore was upset in Super Bowl 3 by Joe Namath and the Jets, Shula was blamed for the loss by owner Carroll Rosenbloom.

The two suffered a rift in their relationship and after Shula coached the team for one more year, he left Baltimore and took over head coaching duties for the Miami Dolphins.

On this particular day, the Dolphins were one game ahead of the Colts, and the upstart Baltimore club was riding a 7-game winning streak. If the Colts won this game, then all they had to do was win the finale the following Sunday and they were miraculously in the playoffs.

Kickoff in Baltimore that day was at 2 PM. American Forces Radio carried the game 'live', which meant I could hear it right there on base in Turkey. That really got me stoked. When the game started, it was 9 PM at Incirlik AFB.

I got prepared for the game with some snacks and a couple of six packs of beer. The contest became a real defensive battle. Miami scored first, and the Colts tied it with minutes to go in regulation.

As the clock struck midnight on Sunday night in Turkey, the game went into overtime.

A little later in overtime, Baltimore's Toni Linhart kicked a field goal and gave the Colts an improbable 10 to 7 victory.

By this time, the snacks were gone, the beer was gone, and I was intoxicated with both the thrill of victory and the effects of alcohol.

By this time, local time was nearly 1 AM. My fellow dorm residents were trying to get some sleep before getting up to go to work on Monday morning. That was a world to which I could not relate at that moment.

Even though I took my portable radio to the dorm room so as not to wake people, I was screaming so loud at the radio and cheering for my hometown team that apparently several folks came to the door and asked me to tone it down.

I then got the idea to go to the pay phone in the barracks and try to call one or two people in Baltimore to share the news. Calls back to the States were tremendously expensive as I have related in an earlier chapter.

Apparently, I could not find a way to connect with anyone and frustration set in. That was the last I remembered, as soon after I made my way back to the room and fell into bed.

The next day, I was asked to come down and meet with the First Sergeant. I had no idea why. After I walked into his office, he immediately explained the reason for our meeting.

'Airman Mathers, you will be given a bill for replacing the pay phone on the second floor. You for some reason ripped it out of the wall overnight. As you can understand, your colleagues are not very happy with you right now as it is the only phone in the entire dorm.'

I replied, 'Sir, I had no idea that I did that.' An explanation was offered as to what happened but it didn't pacify the Sarge.

Another black mark on the record. They were building up. My favorable impressions with several key individuals were rapidly fading away.

I went off base the next day and decided to go Christmas shopping in advance of my flight home. Items purchased included a hookah pipe for my sister Lynda and a Turkish lamp for Mom and Dad.

Mid-week arrived, and on Wednesday December 17th I boarded a plane for Istanbul. This time it was with the complete knowledge and approval of the United States Air Force.

We were heading home and boy, was I excited.

1975: An Incredible Journey

My change in status from active duty to AWOL, August 1975.

CHAPTER TWENTY

BACK IN BALTIMORE

When the Pan Am flight touched down at JFK in New York on a cold and windy day in December, 1975 the first thought that hit me was 'I can't believe I got back here so quickly.'

After clearing customs and walking to the cab stand outside the airport, I passed a long line of pay phones while heading to the door. A man was talking on one of them. Dressed in a dazzling ankle length coat with patent leather white shoes, a white fur collar, shades, jewelry around the neck, and a wide brim fedora.

It occurred to me that Sly Stone of Sly and the Family Stone was deeply engrossed in conversation with somebody. I recognized him, but had no intention of interrupting his call.

On this trip I had a couple of suitcases and money in the pocket. Quite a different scenario from more than 4 months earlier.

The trip down to Baltimore progressed uneventfully and boy was it great to get home. Mom and Dad were a sight for sore eyes and we caught up on a bunch of things from when we last saw each other back in August.

Walt and Lynda each called on the phone and I told them I looked forward to seeing them. Sister Gail lived in Seattle but I had an opportunity to talk to her while I was there.

My stay in Baltimore would be three weeks. The days away would actually place me about 7 days in arrears on leave time with Uncle Sam and I'd have to make that up later. As I was back in reality, none of that mattered then, and I didn't care.

The next day was a Friday and I set out to hitch a ride to Edgewood. Everybody was told about me coming home on leave. Everyone but Muriel. I decided to surprise her.

I told my parents of my intentions and they looked at each other. My father said, 'Boy, she stopped in here on Thanksgiving after going down the street to see her Grandmother. I went down in the cellar to get something and she was hanging all over Jimmy (Lynda's boyfriend). That didn't look good. Be careful.

Those words would come back to haunt me in short order.

My timing was good when I caught a ride on Pulaski Highway from Rosedale to Edgewood. The driver and I made conversation, and then he placed his hand on my knee when we hit Joppatowne (about 3 miles before my destination).

Earlier in the Fall I made a friend at Incirlik with a guy who was friendly enough and we would hang out and drink beer. One such time, he made a move on me and I decked him. He fell on the floor, and I immediately reached down, picked him up, and started to cry and apologized for hitting him.

He just rubbed his jaw and said 'Wow, I didn't expect that.'

We continued hanging out but the relationship was noticeably tempered after that incident.

The driver of the car transporting me to Edgewood was a slightly built fellow and I didn't want a reoccurrence of the aforementioned moment.

I quietly told him that type of thing was not of interest of me and I engaged him back into conversation. It worked. He dropped me off in Edgewood.

It was now 3 PM. To set the scene, here's the irony of what was about to happen.

It's the case of an 18-year old guy who is serving in the military, and about to surprise his girl when she walks off of the school bus after leaving 10th grade at her high school. Two more different worlds perhaps could not have been created.

I walked about 25 yards further down the street from where the bus stopped to let Muriel off. After a few minutes, here comes the bus. My back was turned so she wouldn't see me.

The bus stopped, and kids got off. Then, as if by magic, there she is. My lovely Muriel. Another guy gets off behind her. The bus pulls away. I start to walk toward her, and then….

She turns to the guy behind her, embraces him, and kisses him.

Whoa!

This hit me like a ton of bricks. My first reaction was to slowly approach them. Muriel looked over the guy's shoulder, and got that 'deer in the headlights' look.

I said, 'What is this? Who is he? What is your name?'

'Frank Davis', he replied.

'Frank, this is my girl. We are going to get married. And I don't want you ever putting your hands on her again'

1975: An Incredible Journey

It was Frank's turn to be surprised. He didn't say a word, but quickly walked away. Which left Muriel and I standing alone at the corner of Pulaski Highway and Paul Martin Drive.

My heart was breaking. I knew why I had not received any letters from her since I'd gone back to Turkey. It was because the girl had moved on. My concerns were confirmed.

I must have looked like a fool to anyone in the vicinity, although I don't remember anyone being there. Hands waving, shouting, screaming. I think the emotions of the past year were flooding out in a torrent with this latest development.

Me: 'Do you love him?'

Her: 'I don't know, I don't think so'

Me: 'You never wrote me. Why?'

Her: 'I don't know'

Me: 'We're going down to your house and have a talk'

Her: 'No. Leave me alone.'

I reached over, picked her up, flung her over my shoulder and started down the street toward her house.

Her: 'Let me down'

Me: 'No. I'm gonna have a talk with your mother about this'

We get to the house, I put her down. We are standing out in the driveway shouting. Mom opens the door and wants to know what's going on. So, I give her my side.

Mom then says, 'Muriel, what in the world is going on?'

Muriel then walks past her mother into the house, heads back to her bedroom, goes in and shuts the door.

Mom says, 'Honey I'm really sorry this happened. I don't know what she's thinking, or what she's doing. It seemed to me that things were okay between you two. We were just down there for Thanksgiving and she went up to your house to see everybody.'

Me: 'I am really shocked by what I saw' and then proceeded to share details of the previous 15 minutes or so.

'Muriel, come out here', says Mom.

When she came out of the bedroom and into the living room, Mom says, 'Do you have any idea what you're doing. This boy came home on leave to see you and this is the welcome he gets. I never knew about this Frank kid. Is he the one that lives back in the new section?'

Muriel: 'Yes. I didn't expect him (meaning me) to come here today. Maybe he should have called and let me know'

Me: 'I'm glad I didn't call. Now I know the truth. I was thinking something was wrong. I hadn't heard from you. And now this. You know something? It's better for me to find out because I guess I'll just make different plans for the next three weeks.'

Muriel: 'Are you done with me? I'm going back in the room.'

After she left, I told Mom, 'I have things of mine back there in the bedroom. A stereo, a few other things. And I think I want the ring back that I gave her because it doesn't mean anything anymore. If I can get a ride tomorrow I would like to come up and pick up my stuff and take it down to Brunswick Street.'

Mom: 'I understand. Bobby I am really sorry about this. She doesn't think sometimes and when she gets confused she clams up and won't talk. Sorry, honey. I know this is the last thing you wanted to happen. Maybe tomorrow she'll think different. Meantime, I'll talk to her.

With that, I dejectedly walked down the steps, into the street, and headed up to Pulaski Highway to start the trip back home.

The next day was Saturday. Jimmy Faris had some time to drive me back to Edgewood and retrieve my stereo and a few other things.

When we arrived, I went in and Muriel's mother walked me back to the bedroom.

I started unplugging the stereo and grabbed my tapes and other stuff that belonged to me. It felt like someone died and I was at a funeral. Just couldn't believe it was over.

And then Muriel came into the bedroom, sat down on the bed, and started to cry. She apologized and wanted me to leave everything as it was and let's talk it over.

I could have done that and maybe things would have been different. However, something in my mind told me she really didn't know what she wanted and maybe she needed time to think if she really wanted to be with me. If we were to continue our relationship (which I really wanted) I had to have some kind of assurance.

So, I said, 'I accept your apology but I need to know if you are serious so I am going to take all this home with me. I'll call you later and maybe we can go out and do something together'

She got up and walked out of the room. I loaded everything into Jim's car and back to Baltimore we went.

The next day was Sunday. I hung out at home for a while, and then went out later in the day with Jim over to East Baltimore. I saw the lights at Memorial Stadium from the Harbor Tunnel Thruway and was listening to the Colts and Patriots play. Light snow was falling, the Colts were winning the game and going to the playoffs, and I was very depressed. It would not get better.

Christmas was 4 days away. I had bought presents for Muriel and instead of being with her, I took them down to her grandmother who lived three doors down the street, asking that she pass them on when she sees her.

I spent a lot of time during that leave in Baltimore holed up in my bedroom listening to sad songs and analyzing what went wrong.

Dena, Paul, and Muriel, 1968.

CHAPTER TWENTY-ONE

WORKING THROUGH THE SADNESS

One thing I have never much appreciated in all my years is engaging in pursuits that do not interest me. Some would call that a selfish attitude and they'd likely be right to some degree. Efforts have been made over the years to work on this trait, and simply take the yin with the yang, bro.

In those last days of December, 1975, I mustered up enough energy to try to get out and see people, socialize, and as was my habit back in that day, do it all over beers and music. Try as I might, my heart just wasn't in it. However, the drinking for a time killed the pain and allowed me to focus more on my thoughts. That is, until I passed out from the alcohol. After a few hours of slumber, I at times would grab another can, pop the top, and continue my 'medication'.

Of course, hindsight is 20/20. The events of that time were all hitting me at once which of course tended to distort present reality. Presents for Muriel's family were sitting under the tree. But she was not coming. The decision was made to walk them three doors down the street to Grandmother's house and ask that she give them out when the family visited for the holiday. I did not need to know when they were coming to Grandmom's. Didn't matter, 'cause I knew I wouldn't be there.

Christmas came on a Thursday that year. An unusually quiet day. As the weekend started, I found something that shook me from the doldrums. At least temporarily.

Being a football fan, I sat down with Dad and watched the upstart Baltimore Colts who were miraculously in the NFL Playoffs. It was a Saturday afternoon game in Pittsburgh against the World Champion Steelers. Surprisingly, a number of 'experts' were giving the Colts a good shot to pull the upset. Even Howard Cosell made the Colts a 'Dark Horse' pick to go to the Super Bowl. The game turned into a defensive battle, with both teams tied up 7-7 at the half.

I recall laying on the living room floor, propped up and watching the game. The Colts broke the tie early in the 3rd quarter with a field goal. It was now 10-7. Then the Colts got the ball back and began another drive to the Steeler end zone. The Steelers played somewhat of a sloppy game as the Colts' defense forced five Pittsburgh turnovers.

The Colts were down deep in Steeler territory and looking to go up by 10 points when a Bert Jones pass was intercepted by Mel Blount and just like that, the clock struck 12 for the Cinderella Colts. Pittsburgh immediately went down the field for a go-ahead score and in the remaining moments…added two more touchdowns for good measure. 28-10. That's all she wrote.

My father went upstairs to take a nap, and I grabbed my coat and headed out the door on a cold and windy early evening. The emotional pain had returned even greater as I was a real Colts fan and just like my relationship with a certain girl…their magic carpet ride ended on a bleak note. I felt the loss in more ways than one.

It may have been a marshmallow world in the winter for Dean Martin, but for me the landing pad on that last weekend of 1975 was anything but soft.

The next few days were spent just sitting around talking, listening to music up in the bedroom, taking walks around the neighborhood, and listening to music up in the bedroom. Listened to lots of radio too, and dreamed of the day that perhaps I would be on a Baltimore radio station entertaining the folks.

Finally, on Wednesday the 31st of December, also known as New Year's Eve, my sister's boyfriend Jimmy had at that time rented an apartment in Brooklyn on Jack Street. He asked me to go over with him and help move some belongings around. I had nothing else going on. Sure, let's go.

He picked me up around 10:30 that morning. The drive was about 5 miles. When we got inside, Jim busied himself with his project and invited me to have a glass of bourbon. That was not a good idea. One glass ultimately became the whole bottle and by the time we left his house by mid-afternoon, I was absolutely intoxicated.

Many things were going through my head as we pulled away from Jim's apartment. Foremost in my thoughts was my sad and lonely feeling. I was haunted by the fact that in one week, I would be out of the country, back in Turkey, and would have no shot, even remotely, of winning back my girl.

A plan was hatched in my head. That was usually a dangerous development for me, but as I have said a number of times in telling this story, the Lord directed my steps and skirted me away from disaster. This odyssey would be a classic example of that.

Jim came to a stop at the intersection of Patapsco Avenue and Hanover Street. On impulse, I said, 'Thanks Jimmy, great being with you today. I'm getting out to take care of business'. As I jumped out of the car, I heard Jimmy yell, 'Where you going, man?'

I said, 'I'll catch you later'. I hustled up Hanover Street toward the street. Jim floored the car and headed west. He had to get back to the neighborhood. By this time, the shadows of twilight were overtaking what was left of this late winter's day.

1975: An Incredible Journey

On foot, I traipsed past South Baltimore General Hospital, walked along the outskirts of Cherry Hill (a largely black community that never demonstrated much hospitality to white folks walking through the hood), and after crossing the Hanover Street Bridge over the Middle Branch of the Patapsco River, found myself entering South Baltimore.

It was shared with me that on New Year's Eve, Muriel's family would be visiting with their friends the Sessas at 3135 Fait Avenue in East Baltimore. That was my destination later in the evening. Since the evening was still young, I made my way to kill a little time over in a neighborhood known as Locust Point.

My funds were very limited at that moment and I was saving them for a specific purpose. I had enough for transportation and a few beers. Walking through the brisk wind and in advance of a forecast calling for snow, I arrived at a bar known as Henry's on East Fort Avenue. The street was a long thoroughfare that ended at the famous Fort McHenry, home of the Star Spangled Banner.

Unbeknownst to me, I was soon to be the center of another type of rocket's red glare. After entering Henry's, I walked to the back of the bar (a long narrow venue, situated in a row house as were so many of Baltimore's corner taverns).

The bartender delivered me a mug of cold beer. That beverage, combined with the effects of that bottle of bourbon consumed earlier in the day, induced me to pass out. Yep, went to sleep right there on the stool, hunched over and out like a light.

The next thing I knew, they woke me up and said I could not stay and sleep. I had to leave. So, I stumbled out of the front door and walked around the block in an effort to wake up. Not with much success. It was cold, the night had totally settled in, and as the booze was wearing off…I decided to go back into Henry's.

The bartender shot me a look of irritation but when I produced a dollar, he poured me another beer and told me to stay awake. He asked me where I lived and I was so blitzed all I could do was mumble something that made no sense. Well, I drank half of the beer and went to the men's room. I locked the door, sat down on the pot, and went to sleep.

Sometime later, they pounded on the door and I finally roused up enough to open it. Ever seen a line of angry drinkers who couldn't use the men's room and were doing their best to 'hold it'? That is what we had. My pants were not down nor in the process of using the facility. I was simply sleeping.

After they got me out of there, one of them walked me to the door, escorted me out, and said, 'Go home and sleep it off!' I repeated the same around the block walk, checked the time, and it was still too early (in my mind) to implement the rest of my plan.

Naturally, I went back into Henry's to get warm. This time, their patience had run out. Those South Baltimore lads can be tough when they want to be. The fellas in Henry's that night had had enough of me. Likely I said something that was not taken well and next I knew, I was taken to the door and thrown down the steps to the sidewalk.

I sat up on the sidewalk and looked around. By this time snow was falling, giving the scene an eerie stillness which to me meant sadness. Boy, did I feel all alone at that time. I got to my feet, looked across Fort Avenue and noticed the glow of the sign standing above the Coca-Cola bottling plant, illuminated by the curtain of white against the street lights.

I had enough of Henry's inhospitality and if you were to get their side of the story, they had long before tired of my act. I walked to a phone booth and called a cab. When the driver arrived, I asked him to take me to 3135 Fait Avenue in East Baltimore.

The drive from here to there was no more than 25 minutes, and I sat in the back of the warm cab alone with my thoughts. How did I get to this point in my life? It had been quite a year. I didn't feel I belonged anywhere anymore. Like a Man Without a Country (thank you, Edward Everett Hale).

As the cab pulled up in front of the house, I reached over and gave the driver every penny I had, He took my offering, mumbled something like 'at least we got you off the street'. I said, 'Sir that is all I have. Thanks for bringing me here'. I got out, he drove off, and I walked up to the marble steps of the house and rapped on the door.

A shadowy figure behind the curtains looked out, and then whomever that person was, stepped back into the house and the next thing I knew…Muriel's mother and her friend Honey were standing there with their mouths open.

Muriel's mother instantly felt pity for me and asked, 'Where have you been, Bobby? You look like you've been in a war'. I then realized the boys at Henry's must have pounded on me a little bit and left a few marks. 'Get in here out of the cold'.

I walked in, said hi to everyone, and noticed Muriel over in the corner. She didn't make an effort to greet me, or say hi, or anything. She was in shock. Probably never expected to see me anytime soon, if ever again. Dena on the other hand, shook her head and said, 'Bobby, what in the world are you doing?'

In a little while, I warmed up from being in the cold and grabbed a seat around the table watching the adults play cards and telling them of my adventures that day and evening. Muriel actually pulled up a chair and sat next to me. That really surprised me.

We were approaching midnight and in the waning moments of 1975, prepared to usher in the new year with fireworks and pots and pans. Real Baltimore style to say the least.

They all went outside and celebrated the arrival of 1976. I laid prone on the sofa celebrating a warm home. This sleeping environment felt a lot better than the bar stool at Henry's. And, a lot more hospitable.

Next, I was roused up by Muriel's mom who said, 'You're in no condition to go home to Brunswick Street. We're taking you with us up to our house. You can get a good night's sleep and head home tomorrow. Gary will take you back then.' I thanked her for her kindness and when it was time to leave, I piled into back of the car and sat with Muriel. Whatever my convoluted plan was at the start of the day, the efforts brought success as I was now next to the girl I loved.

For one last hurrah, we were a couple. And even though she was treating me affectionately on the way home, I knew in my heart of hearts it would be goodbye. The events of the next few days would bear that out.

Brother Walt and friend Rick Thomas.

CHAPTER TWENTY-TWO

ADIOS BALTIMORE, HELLO INCIRLIK

As the new hours of a new year unfolded on Thursday January 1, 1976…I was lying flat on my back ready to fall asleep with Muriel by my side holding me. At that moment, the world was right. The girl I loved since she was 9 lay there in my arms as I rambled on about a number of things.

It turned out that her gesture was not one of reconciliation, but goodbye. She didn't even have to say it. I knew it.

The next day as I awoke and made my way to the kitchen, there was a strange silence about the place. Of course, New Year's Day for the celebrant is usually that way. For me, the atmosphere took on a different significance.

Throughout the day, I noticed Muriel was avoiding me and didn't seem interested in having conversation. Efforts to have any kind of meaningful discussion were met mostly with silence. By the end of the day my depression had returned. There just wasn't anything left between us anymore. The spark, or whatever it was, had died. The love was gone. It was time for me to go as well.

Just after dark, Gary asked me, 'Are you ready?'. This is what a condemned man must feel like when they come to lead him to the gallows or the chair. I said, 'I am'. I don't remember if I hugged anybody when I left. This was so long ago. I studied their faces and said to myself, 'You may never see these people again and they have been so good to you'.

Truly I didn't know what I was going to miss more. Muriel's companionship and love, or the family relationship that grew through the past 18 months with her parents, sister, and brother. I think in an odd sort of way, it was the second thing that I lamented more. The romance with Muriel had been gone for months. Ever since the AWOL days with the money splurge at the baseball game, and cemented by the surprise at the bus stop just before Christmas. The trust was no longer there.

Gary May was Muriel's stepfather. His relationship with the stepchildren according to what I was told years later was at times very contentious. To me, Gary May was a good man. A kind mans. A sympathetic man. A compassionate man.

On the way down, I-95 as he drove me back to Brunswick Street, he offered to pull off the interstate, stop at a tavern on O'Donnell Street and buy me a beer. He knew I had a lot of pent-up emotions inside and it was his way of offering me an ear to listen and offer insight as to maybe why things turned out the way they did.

Man, did I pour out my heart. I kept asking 'Why is she so cold? What did I do wrong? What could I have done differently? Is there anything I can do now to change the outcome? Gary listened patiently for a long time, and then proceeded to give his take.

'Bob, first of all, she's only 15 years old. You're only 18 yourself but you have seen and done a lot more than she has. Maybe there'll come a time in the future when she comes around to try to see it your way and come back together, but obviously not now.'

'Her mother talked to her. I talked to her. Even her grandmother talked to her. She is very stubborn and when that's the case, no use in trying further. All I can say is I'm sorry all of this happened to you at this particular time. Let's stay in touch and if things change at some point, we'll all know. Meanwhile, you're going back to Turkey next week and I wish you well, and hope that everything works out for you.'

'It was nice seeing you again and although it doesn't feel like it now, Happy New Year'

We resumed our drive to Southwest Baltimore and I got out of the car. After shaking Gary's hand, he drove away. I watched the red tail lights on the chocolate covered Plymouth head up Brunswick Street and turn the corner, out of sight.

The next day was Friday and time to collect my thoughts and prepare to return to Turkey. It was very nice of the brass back at the base to allow me a leave when at the time I was in arrears on time off because of the AWOL experience and actually owed the government for taking excess time away.

The last weekend at home was quiet. My spirits were still low but I realized thanks to pep talks from Mom and Dad that the recent developments were not the end of the world, that things in the relationship with Muriel were not meant to be, and that I had my whole life ahead of me and to just set goals and be the best I could be.

Good advice for sure. I would be smart to take it.

Monday, January 5th dawned bright and sunny. My duffle bag was packed and Mom drove me to Penn Station in downtown Baltimore to jump on the Amtrak for New York. The ride up was uneventful except for the stop in Edgewood. I knew I'd be passing the scene of my last visit. So be it. Sure, it hurt but like the folks said, it's not forever.

It's really strange how when you get wrapped up in a love affair and it ends on terms other than those of your choosing, the feeling of rejection is so strong that for a time, you can't envision loving anyone else again. Also, when you're in that situation, and you don't have the Lord Jesus in your life, the feeling of sadness simply engulfs you.

However, the Lord says in the scriptures in Jeremiah 29:11. 'For I know the plans I have for you. They are plans for good, and not evil. For hope, and for a purpose.'

I was sharing with someone just the other day about the events of 1975 and how they shaped my life. Had I taken a different direction out of high school, like going to college for broadcasting, or securing an internship at a Baltimore radio station, none of what you have read would have even happened.

But it did.

As the train was pulling into New York City, my thoughts were on returning to Turkey to see what could be done with my need to acclimate to Air Force life. As I boarded the plane, I had no option but to continue to work through things and simply move on.

As the big Pan Am jet cruised across the Atlantic, I took stock of where I was and then and there determined to work through the challenges that lay before me. And there were a few.

First was the mental aspect. I had abandoned any hope of ever repairing that relationship. I was now to her as I had been for the better part of the last year. Out of sight, out of mind. All that happened in the last few weeks was a cameo appearance. Essentially, Bob came back into Muriel's life for the final breakup and to say goodbye. I just didn't see how we were ever going to get back together again, 'cause I'd be gone for a long time...and 9 months is a lifetime in a 16-year old's life. Hers, that is. I would be quickly forgotten...and I had no choice but to accept that.

Next was the bigger issue. My career. Because key personnel in authority were gracious enough to allow me to volunteer at the AFRTS station on base, that daily experience helped me to 'accept' the

Computer Operator position assigned to me by the Air Force. However, it wasn't enough to satisfy. I knew that when my tour in Turkey was over in September, my next assignment would likely be in the US. Where they do not have AFRTS broadcasts as those stations were outside the lower 48.

What then? I would likely stay 100% with the computers and when my 4 years in the military were complete, either re-up to train as a broadcaster or separate at 21 and try to find something on the outside in civilian life.

The best course of action was to not to look too far ahead and somehow immerse myself into life at Incirlik. After all, there were people there who also would have preferred to be back home, but they worked with what they were given and adjusted quite well. For some reason, I had a hard time trying to do that.

In retrospect, I placed way too much value on living in Baltimore and the environment that I came out of. I was born and raised in the inner city and enjoyed many wonderful moments there. Yet, the culture was one of drinking and partying, no commitment, and being always on the move. With me, it was radio, baseball, girls (one), and beer.

The opportunity to go back and reacquaint myself with what I thought I missed during both the AWOL period and the authorized end-of-year leave reminded me of why I made the decision to go into the Air Force and learn a career. Had they granted me the chance to test for broadcasting/journalism, I believed I would have passed it and then set my path in that manner. But we will never know the answer.

When I returned to Incirlik, a number of my colleagues feigned surprise when they saw me, and joked about the fact that I actually returned back to Turkey on my own. The first couple of weeks back went well enough. The computer duties were now more easily understood and my supervisors were pleased at the level of competence I showed in mastering more and more of the job.

So, pleased that they moved me to the overnight shift as Supervisor in a three-person crew. I think I was more surprised than they were. In my mind I was still feeling a bit emotionally fragile, and the façade of confidence they saw in me was just that. Although my world began to settle down and improve, I still felt a lot of pain about the other world. The one I left behind at the beginning of the month.

By the end of January, cracks were beginning to show up in my mental stability. For the life of me, I decided to isolate myself and drink copious amounts of alcohol. Or if I did go out and socialize, it was by spending evenings at the NCO Club where I pounded booze in all varieties. Mostly beer, but every other spirit as well.

One such evening, I was in the NCO Club and playing the pinball machine. I was eating an appetizer and drinking my beer when I started feeling bored. When that occurs, watch out. I walked away from the pinball machine and moved over to the bar.

I then motioned the bartender over and asked him how much the cost would be if he took a water glass and poured into that glass…a shot of every single bottle behind the bar, mixed it up, and served it to me? He said something along the lines of 10.00 for the glass which in mid-70's military discounted dollars were somewhat hefty.

I asked him to do it. He did. I drank it down. The next thing I remember, I was crawling along the sidewalk on my hands and knees in front of the base post office. That is all I remember before waking up in bed late that night with a terrible hangover.

I couldn't move. So much so, I didn't make it to work and was considered AWOL.

This episode started a chain of events that placed me on the road to even greater notoriety around the base. It would get a lot worse before it got better.

1975: An Incredible Journey

Me and Muriel today.

CHAPTER TWENTY-THREE

SPIRALING DOWNWARD

By mid-January of 1975, just two short weeks after returning to duty after my Baltimore visit, yours truly was digging himself a deep pit of trouble. The alcohol intended to 'medicate' my rapidly deepening depression was of course, creating an environment that accelerated my decline.

From the outside looking in, Airman Robert Mathers was a baffling case study. The young man who just turned 18 showed flashes of talent and intelligence to his superiors, and treated people generally in a very kind manner. Yet a darker side of the individual was emerging and it was discovered later that many in authority around the base were discussing how to handle me.

Following that episode at the NCO Club and subsequent efforts to get home that evening, I began to drink even more heavily to the point of blacking out. Waking up from a load-on and not remembering what I did, where I went, or who I spoke to. It didn't matter. Others were witness to the bad behavior and they did not like it at all.

My immediate supervisor Sergeant Wells was a most patient and caring man, even to the point of excusing that first incident of UA (chalking it up to sickness), but after that I got no breaks. Nor should I have gotten any. It's not easy to recall one's emotions with total accuracy nearly 50 years in the past, but one clear memory that has stayed with me was how angry I felt about being turned down for a transfer to AFTRTS and the point was reached where I just didn't care anymore.

Thanks to my military records retrieved from the National Personnel Records Center, there is no confusion about the series of incidents that rapidly followed throughout January.

On Friday January 23rd, little more than two weeks after arriving back at Incirlik, I failed to show up for work. I passed out Thursday night after plowing through well over a dozen cans of beer and several water glasses full of rum and coke. When the clock struck midnight to begin the Friday overnight shift, this boy was out of it.

That offense in and of itself earned me the vacation of probation imposed in September 1975 for being AWOL in the prior month. Meaning, I was now officially busted down to E-1 Airman Basic retroactive to the previous September.

But there was more to come.

Apparently in one of my last volunteer shifts at the AFRTS base before losing THAT privilege, I commandeered a few albums from the station library to take back to the barracks and enjoy while getting drunk. This was discovered by personnel and that along with my showing up there highly intoxicated one day (not to work, but to retrieve the recordings) sealed the deal for separating Bob Mathers from the Incirlik AFRTS.

On Wednesday January 28, I was out for the evening and returning to the dorm could not locate my keys. I was locked out. So according to the military records…

'Preliminary information has disclosed that you did, at Incirlik CDI, without proper authority, willfully destroy by breaking a chair of a value of $29.90, military property of the United States, in violation of Article 108. Further preliminary investigation has revealed that you also, willfully damage by breaking a hole in the door and breaking the inner door knob off of said door, a value of $75.00, the amount of said damage being the sum of about $15.00.

On Thursday January 29, I failed to show up for work because after breaking into the room as detailed in the above paragraph, I went out like a light.

To this day, I don't remember any of that. Quite frankly, I've no doubt that it happened because I just didn't care anymore. I wanted to get out and go home and in my mind, I didn't care what the Air Force wanted to do to me. I totally gave up on any possibility that I could turn this thing around.

One day later I was summoned to Captain Clark's office to account for these violations.

As I have said before, Gregory C. Clark was a very kind and friendly man. He saw something in me that gave him reason to help me overcome my personal demons. He tried his best. In the ensuing years I have tried to look him up but with no success thus far. He would probably take at least some small satisfaction that I made good on my vow to enter broadcasting, considering I've been doing this line of work for a long time.

Nevertheless, even his patience had limits. We had a talk and he said to me that if I was willing to give the Air Force a full commitment, he would be willing to not only change the decision on the reduction to Airman Basic, but would actually authorize my promotion to Airman First Class and promote me into a greater position of responsibility at the Computer Center.

My response (and I say this to my enduring shame and regret) was to tell him, 'Thank you, sir, but I just want to get out of here and I don't care what kind of a discharge I get, if I have to hit you in the head to bring charges, I would.'

The Captain sat there and fixed his gaze upon me. His jaw was clenched and I thought to myself 'Well, you asked for it, dummy'. Then after a couple of seconds of thought, he straightened up in his chair and said, 'Alright. I have done what I can do. There's nothing else I can do. I am going to authorize a discharge.

'I don't believe you are the violent type but you are certainly the desperate type and it is my view that you are no longer capable of adjusting to military life. Because of your basically kind nature in spite of the stunts you have pulled and the stupid things you seem bent on doing to ruin your career and perhaps the rest of your life, my feeling is I'm not going to destroy you with a decision of giving you a Dishonorable Discharge.

'I'm going to see to it that you receive an Honorable Discharge because I believe you are sincere in wanting broadcasting so badly that you would take it to this extreme. I do believe that had you gotten an opportunity in basic to pass or fail application for entrance into broadcast communications, things may have turned out differently. But anybody that has put himself through what you have over the last 9 months must have quite a burning passion for radio. Either that, or you've done a good job in snowing us all and I don't think it's that.

'As soon as the paperwork is completed, you will be removed from active duty and placed in a holding status. You are confined to the base and are advised to stay on the grounds of the Squadron. You will report to the First Sergeant and serve at his discretion with whatever chores and directives he orders you to do around the dorm.

'One more thing. This decision is subject to revision before it becomes official. If you commit additional offenses or are even seen in an inebriated state between now and the time you process out of here, you'll wish you had never drunk a drop of alcohol.

'Am I clear?'

Alcoholics Anonymous couldn't have gotten a man off the bottle any faster than that last statement did for me. I looked at him with tears in my eyes and said, 'Yes sir. Thank you, sir.' It was like a one-ton load had been taken off my back. I then asked him how long the process would take?

He replied, 'Usually about one to two weeks. The paperwork has to go through the process so we can't say for sure.'

With that, the meeting adjourned and I went back to the dorm to sit, reflect, and ponder the future. At least with this news, I felt like I had a future.

My departure from the computer room where I had more or less worked over the past 6 months was barely noticed. Not one thing do I remember in the way of a goodbye or even a good riddance. Could I blame them? Absolutely not.

In looking back at this period of my life, I have an exceptionally good name recall of people who figure prominently in this story, and in some cases only in passing. However, I do not remember the name of the First Sergeant to whom I reported during the remaining days of my Air Force tenure.

He is remembered as a kind and patient man. A Senior Master Sergeant with a craggy countenance and quiet manner. That served me in good stead because at this time in my military career (or what was left of whatever that career was), I was to my everlasting shame an uncooperative lad.

Here's an example. There were a couple of other guys in the barracks who shared my status. One such fellow was James Grimes. One day the two of us were directed to walk around through all of the hallways, check outlets for safety, and room doors for security.

It is not recalled how it happened, but Grimes and I for some reason on that particular day, began arguing about how we were supposed to carry out this 'make work' assignment. The bickering ensued until Grimes pulled a switchblade and began to threaten me.

I digress here to say that Grimes was a black man, and having grown up in the inner city of Baltimore, my acquired street sense took hold. Before I continue with how the incident concluded, let me say that regardless of what color a person is, when you're raised in a neighborhood that is all one race, and then the community adjacent to that is mostly a different race, the racial aspect comes into play pretty quickly.

During those growing up years, I happened to have a number of guys who were good friends and I liked hanging with them. They just happened to be black. Thus, it was not a prejudice thing with me. However, it was a cultural issue when race created the conflict more often than not…and memories remain of some rather tense encounters from back in the day.

I looked at Grimes, then looked down at the knife, then back to Grimes, and said to him, 'If you come at me with that blade, I will take it from you, and then I will break your neck'.

His expression was one of surprise. He took a step back, calmly folded the knife and put it away, and apologized. He extended his hand. I shook it, and said, 'It's okay. I probably said something that angered you so we were both wrong. I also apologize. Let's forget it.' We finished the task at hand and got along fine during the remaining time.

Several weeks went by and I wasn't hearing anything about my discharge. Not a peep. Captain Clark told me seven days, and later after arriving home, my parents showed me a hand-written letter from Clark informing them of my impending discharge and gave them the same time frame for my separation.

The boredom was beginning to get to me, but I remembered Captain Clark's admonition to stay away from trouble. I knew alcohol would certainly create that trouble and yours truly didn't go anywhere near the NCO Club or to a Class Six store to make a purchase.

So, I bided my time for a while. Did a lot of reading and starting formulating plans about how I was going to get into broadcasting after arriving back in the states and transitioning back to civilian life. There would be much training required as my volunteer work at AFRTS was behind-the-scenes on the TV side.

Finally, I decided I had better go and see the Captain to ask why my discharge was being held up. The answer I received explained the delay.

1975: An Incredible Journey

REQUEST AND AUTHORIZATION FOR SEPARATION

1. TYPE OF SEPARATION: ☒ DISCHARGE	2. AUTHORITY: By Order of the Secretary of the Air Force	
3. GRADE, NAME AND SSAN: AB MATHERS, ROBERT H. 218-70-5659	4. PLACE OF ENTRY ON ACTIVE DUTY: Baltimore MD	5. HOME OF RECORD: 506 Brunswick St., Baltimore MD 21223
		6. FUTURE MAILING ADDRESS: Same as HOR
8. YOE: 1957	9. PAFSC: 51150A	12. DATE OF RANK: 11 Feb 1976
15. MEMBER IS: ☒ DISCHARGED	16. EFFECTIVE DATE: 12 Mar 1976	18. TYPE OF DISCHARGE: ☒ HONORABLE
		19. CERTIFICATE NUMBER: DD Form 256AF
21. RELIEVED FROM ASSIGNMENT: TUSLOG Det 10 (USAFE) APO NY 09289 W/DY this stn, CBPO: 438 ABG (MAC) (MNOQFCMJ) MCGUIRE AFB NEW JERSEY 08641	22. WILL PROCEED TO: ☒ HOME OF RECORD	

26. REMARKS: TRANSPORTATION OFFICER will furnish transportation in kind to HOR or another place as requested by AB MATHERS, ROBERT H., 218-70-5659 and approved by Unit Commander as long as cost does not exceed that to HOR or POE.

27. DATE: 12 Mar 1976	28. ORDERS ISSUING/APPROVING OFFICIAL: E.F. WOOD, MSGT, USAF, Chief Port Separation Facility	29. SIGNATURE: /s/ E.F. Wood

30. EXPENSES CHARGEABLE TO: 5763500 326 048 5881.0M S503725
NONTEMPORARY STORAGE CHARGEABLE TO: 5763500 326 048 5888.0N S503725

31. DESIGNATION AND LOCATION OF HEADQUARTERS: DEPARTMENT OF THE AIR FORCE HQ 438TH MILITARY AIRLIFT WING (MAC) MCGUIRE AFB NEW JERSEY 08641	32. AUTHORITY: AFM 39-10	33. SO NO: AB-482	34. DATE: 12 Mar 1976
	35. TDN PCS: FOR THE COMMANDER		
36. DISTRIBUTION: "A"	37. SIGNATURE ELEMENT OF ORDERS AUTHENTICATING OFFICIAL: /s/ E.F. Wood E.F. WOOD, MSGT, USAF Asst Chief of Administration		

AF FORM 100 JUL 76 PREVIOUS EDITION IS OBSOLETE

My separation papers. March 1976.

CHAPTER TWENTY-FOUR

ONE MORE HURDLE

February is the shortest month of the year. Even when leap year comes around and adds an extra day (1976 was a leap year), that makes 29 days.

I decided about three weeks into the month that since I hadn't heard from anybody about my discharge, I'd better start looking into it. There was a growing sense that something or someone was dragging their feet. Thus, I stopped by Captain Clark's office, and he agreed to see me.

The Captain said he had no answers for me, but that he would check on it and get back to me. The following day, he summoned me to come in. He had an update for me.

When I arrived, he seemed a little frustrated. When he gave me an update, I understood why? 'I called Major 'so-and-so' up at Personnel and asked him where the discharge was. He replied, 'I haven't done anything since you sent me the request.

The Major continued, 'I have looked into Airman Mathers' background and honestly, he isn't deserving of an Honorable Discharge. It is my opinion that he should get no more than a General under Honorable Discharge, maybe just a General, and if it were up to me, Mathers would get an Undesirable.'

Clark explained to the Major that he was not going to alter the decision. The Major said to me, 'I'm a Major. You're a Captain. I have rank here'. Clark told him, 'But Mathers is under my direct authority and I have the final say.'

The Major up at Personnel agreed that was the case, but obviously he was letting the paperwork sit. He wasn't even slow walking it through the process. I asked the Captain what could be done. He advised me to be patient and he would stay on it.

After leaving his office, I got an idea. When Bob Mathers gets an idea, it can sometimes be productive if he has a clear goal in mind. And in this case, I certainly had one. It was a Sunday, and I decided to take a walk across the base to the Personnel Building. I walked through the front door and because it was a weekend, no brass were present. There was basically a skeleton crew and it took me a while to find someone I could talk with.

Finally, I located a nice and personable red-headed Sergeant sitting behind a desk. Her cute and bubbly manner gave me an assurance I could level with her. She saw me, looked up and said with a smile, 'How can I help you?' I flashed her a smile and said 'How are you doing?' She replied, 'Anyway I can!'

I laughed at her answer, then introduced myself and asked her if she had any information on a discharge application for Airman Robert H. Mathers. I posed my question without telling her who I was. It is not recalled that she asked me who I was.

However, as she was rummaging through the paperwork in an effort to help me, I talked with her and said the following.

'I am Robert Mathers, and the reason I am here is because I was supposed to be processed out of Turkey and sent back to the States over a week ago. Today is Sunday and I figured I could get a quick update without distracting anybody.'

She stared at me for a minute, and then with a smile, said, 'I understand. Let me see what I have here.' After about 5 minutes of checking, she paused, looked up and said, 'For some reason, your paperwork has been on hold for a while. I'm not sure why that is, but I can tell you all of your packages are sitting up at the photography building.

Apparently, before they finish the process, they need to take a picture of you to go with everything.'

I asked her where that facility was located on the base. After she gave me directions, I flashed her a smile and thanked her for being so kind and helpful. She smiled back and said, 'Good luck!'

Moments later I walked through the door of the next stop and talked with a guy there.

Much like the redhead back at Personnel, he was the only one in the place. I told him who I was, and why I was there. He flashed me a suspicious look, and I quickly added, 'Why not call down to personnel and ask for the Sergeant on Duty? That cute redhead who I talked with about a half an hour ago. She'll tell you about our conversation.

He did just that, and sure enough, she verified my visit. He thanked her, hung up the phone, and a narrowing squint in his eye, said, 'I'm not sure I'm supposed to do this, but in looking over these papers they have been here an awfully long time.

I asked, 'Well would you like to take the picture now?' He did, and then I asked him, 'How about if I can hand carry this to the next stop?' He told me where to take it, placed the package in my hands, and bid me a great day.

So, as it occurred to me I was handling my own discharge and learning about red tape and stalemates, I was left with the feeling that someone upstairs was not in my corner and holding up the deal.

My suspicions proved right. The Major in Personnel was deeply disturbed that yours truly was in his view, 'pulling a fast one on this man's Air Force' and decided to slow walk the paperwork, which in effect kept me in limbo until everything was ready.

Therefore, I not only dropped the package off at the next station, I told the recipient to look at the filing date and understand how long it was taking to get this done. He agreed and then proceeded to share with me what steps remained and how many people had to sign off to finalize the discharge and get me out of the country.

So, in effect, I walked my discharge papers through every remaining stop in the process. If I sensed things had bogged down, I would make a discreet query to someone at the agency that had access to the documents and they would if needed, get the ball moving again.

Finally, the day came when Captain Clark called me in and told me the papers were approved and I was due to fly out within a week. We talked in some detail about the way things had transpired to that point and he again reiterated that the Major at Personnel tried one more time to amend my discharge to a General under Honorable Conditions. That is a level just under Honorable, and above General. The other levels of separation are Undesirable and Dishonorable.

He also shared with me a letter he wrote and mailed to my parents in Baltimore expressing regret about their son's inability to adapt to military life. I told him, 'It's ironic Captain Clark. The two most satisfying and fulfilling times of my brief time in the Air Force were Basic Training and Tech School. It's usually in Basic that people are weeded out and returned to civilian life and it's because of their 'inability to adapt'.'

I added, 'A career counselor in Basic asked if I had ever abused substances. I replied there were 4 times that I knew of where I smoked marijuana and only one occasion where I took a pill not knowing what it was. His reply was 'We can get you out of here with an Honorable Discharge right now. Just tell us, because we need to know if there would be a reoccurrence of this and if so, we could have problems with you down the line.'

'When I told the counselor at Lackland that I refused the honorable discharge and would rather stay in the Air Force, he noted the decision and the interview ended. I remembered the feeling of satisfaction upon returning to the squadron and telling them I turned down the opportunity to leave. It was at that point that I felt a growing respect from my fellow recruits, who congratulated me on doing so, and thus looked on that as having made the right decision and 'manning up' to the challenge.

More than a few recruits opted out right there and then and went home. I was not one of them.'

Having said this to the Captain, he shook his head, smiled, and said 'I never knew that.' Clark added, 'With that being the case, why has it been so difficult for you to adjust to military life which for the most part entails a career, a job, and opportunity to rise in the ranks and advance yourself?'

My reply was something like, 'Sir, I know what I want to do with my career and it is important to me to get on with it. If I were to have stayed in the Air Force after discovering that I could have trained for broadcasting in basic training but was never even given the chance, I would feel like I'm throwing away years of my life operating computers. And when Sergeant Ennis vetoed Sergeant Indianer's request to have me transfer from Data to AFRTS just because he didn't like me and felt I had been given enough slack, that did it for me.'

Clark said, 'Bob I wish you all the best. You'll be flying a civilian instead of a military flight from Adana to Istanbul, and then on the Pan Am international run to JFK. You'll be met after passing through customs by MP's from McGuire Air Force Base. They will escort you to the base where you will be processed out of the service and then given transportation home to Baltimore.'

There really wasn't much to pack. I never acquired much during my time at Incirlik and the items that were purchased had already been taken back to Baltimore during my leave less than 90 days prior.

Everything fit in a green military issue duffle bag. I neatly packed my dress blues and fatigues and was set to go. I dressed in civvies for the flight back to the States.

On 4 March 1976, the die was cast. On 8 March 1976, the day had come. It was a Monday, and no Monday ever looked so good to me as that one did.

When I awoke that morning and went to the chow hall for some breakfast (my last meal as it were in Turkey), my thoughts understandably shifted to the future after returning home. As I was mulling over the what ifs and goals that lie ahead, it occurred to me that I was truly on the receiving end of a miracle. An opportunity to 'get it right' with my passionate desire to launch a career in broadcasting.

The remainder of the time prior to riding to the airport in Adana flew by in a blur. My emotions were not so much feelings of joy, but more so of relief. As I recall, the only person to whom I said farewell was Captain Clark. That man did so much for me and he was a fellow that I liked and appreciated. We mutually wished each other well and shook hands.

As I boarded the plane in Adana and rode the big jet on the way to Istanbul, the events of the past year began to play back through my mind like a movie. Those thoughts brought a deep sense of relief that served as the start of a healing process that unbeknownst to me would go on for many years to come.

After arriving in Istanbul for what was my third flight back to the States in the past 9 months (I was becoming an old hand at this process), unlike the other journeys, the wait was much shorter before the final flight arrived. When I settled in my seat on the Pan Am flight, the peace that came over me was indescribable.

1975: An Incredible Journey

I was heading home. For good.

1975: An Incredible Journey

DEPARTMENT OF THE AIR FORCE
HEADQUARTERS SHEPPARD TECHNICAL TRAINING CENTER (ATC)
SHEPPARD AIR FORCE BASE TEXAS 76311

SPECIAL ORDER 7 May 1975
AD-2199

ASGN: Ea of the fol AB (E-1) (CAFSC indicated) rlvd fr Stu Sq indicated (PL Stu) ATC Sheppard AFB TX 76311; asgnd orgn indicated. Non-Vol unless otherwise indicated.
Scty Clnc - None. TED Jun 75.
RPRT DATA: DDALVP.
GEN INSTRUC: Auth: AFR 39-11 and PCS Code "J". Upon grad fr Crs indicated, award PAFSC indicated. Amn will rprt to TMO, Bldg 402, Room 251, NLT 3 days prior to dep for issuance of MTA/TR. Mbr will comply with rprt time and flt reservations in the MTA (DD Form 1482) or as arngd by the TMO per AFM 75-8, atch 1, and is not authd to dep this stn before rcpt of validated MTA (DD Form 1482) or GTR (SF 1169) fr the TMO. Rprt to I&OP, Stn 1, Bldg 402, Room 112 for final off-base clnc NET dt of dep. Traveler is rqrd to subm a tvl vou within 5 WD after compl of tvl.
TRNSP: Amn will normally dep NLT day fol grad. (Anticipated grad dt 29 May 75) PCS. TDN. 5753500 325 5871.0* S503725 CIC: 4 5 548 0070 503725 TAC: F58D.(* Insert M for Mbr; D for Depn; H for HHG (GB/L); L for DLA) TPC with permitted tvl time indicated.

Crs 3ABR51130A; PDS Code AHC; CAFSC and PAFSC 51130A
TUSLOG Det 175, APO New York 09289 (PAS INOQFCTZ) 5 days tvl time

ROBERT H MATHERS, 218-70-5659(LNAC Mar 75) 3755 Stu Sq (PAS SQOJFCKB)
AAN 0650NS2966 Lv adrs - 506 Brunswick, Baltimore MD 21223

The actual document that got me out of Turkey and into New York. Dated May 1975, it served me well three months later.

CHAPTER TWENTY-FIVE

MCGUIRE AND DONE

The Pan Am flight touched down at John F. Kennedy airport in Brooklyn, New York in the early evening of 9 March 1976. After clearing customs, I was met by a couple of guys from McGuire Air Force Base who walked me to the bus waiting outside of the terminal. There were other military personnel who arrived on the same flight and were also heading to my destination.

The bus ride covered nearly 90 miles and took the better part of two hours. McGuire is a sprawling complex just east of the New Jersey Turnpike in suburban Trenton. I was shown to a transient barracks to bed down for the night and given instructions where to report the following day.

Next came a lesson to me about patience, something I have always had a challenge with.

When I reported to the office that handled my separation, it was my expectation that I'd be out of there later in the day. My hopes of quickly mustering out were dashed after the man handling my case went over everything that had to happen before my departure.

It was emphasized that regardless of my imminent discharge, I was still the property of the United States Air Force. The government had to research my record to make sure I had no outstanding charges against me or no outstanding debts owed to Uncle Sam. There were classes to learn of my benefits and rights after separation. All of this would take time, most likely a couple of days.

I protested to one of the officials my irritation of having to 'hang around' the base wasting time and immediately received a stern rebuke. It was deserved. So, I piped down and went along with the program.

The March weather was chilly and windy during my brief stay at McGuire. During one of a series of meetings with personnel processing my separation, I was asked about a note in my records stating I owed the US Air Force leave time. My response was one of curiosity, in which it was pointed out the unique aspects of my absence from active duty in the past 9 months and how it came to be that way. How much?

When the various aspects of the leave imbalance were hashed out, the Sergeant who was conducting the interview told me in so many words that yours truly owed the US Government money to pay back the overage. When the questioner was told no money existed to make restitution as I brought nothing back with me to the States but my clothing and what personal items were packed, he told me they would deduct the money from whatever final pay was owed to me.

Turns out after they appropriated my last check, I still owed the US seven days excess leave. When I asked how I intended to pay it, my answer was simply, 'I can't. I'm broke'. They tried for a couple of months after that asking for it but every time my answer was I had no money. Finally, by the summer I heard no more from them. Even so, my separation document (DD 214) still to this day shows 'Owes US 7 days excess leave'.

The last thing on my mind at that time was money. The Air Force guaranteed me finances to return to Baltimore and for me, that was enough. Even so, the prospect of owing the 'gummint' money was not at all appealing. All I wanted to do was separate from this experience quickly and completely.

The process continued on with a series of debriefings for the few of us who were mustering out of the military. Things like how to readjust to civilian life, various ways to take advantage of veteran benefits, important phone numbers for post career counselors, and the like.

This part of the exit proceedings was one that I embraced enthusiastically. Although it has been nearly 50 years later as I pen this memoir, the emotions and scenarios of those last few hours are recalled by this writer as if it were only yesterday.

12 March 1976 dawned cloudy, windy, and cold. A gloom hung in the air. Almost as if it would snow at any minute. For me, the day was one of joy and expectation. I assembled with the others for a final meeting. There we were handed transportation vouchers that would take us to our various destinations.

My exodus was a simple one. I didn't have far to go. About 130 miles from the Amtrak Train Station in Trenton to Penn Station in Baltimore. More or less a 2-hour ride via the rails. A part of that route would send me back on the same one taken just 9 weeks before. That sad and lonely January day seemed as if it were 9 years ago. So much had changed in that period of time.

All that was left was to gather my belongings into my duffle bag and report to the point of exit that would take me to the train station. Dressed in civilian clothes, the only military issue clothing packed in that bag was a field jacket and a shirt, both tagged with my last name. Every other item, from work uniforms to a set of dress blues, were placed into the bottom of the closet and left for whomever would retrieve them to do with it as they saw fit.

As I exited the building, the chill in the air hit me hard and the wind blew in my face as I walked west across the field to the van that would serve as my ride to the train station. The steel gray sky lent a sort of melancholy atmosphere to the proceedings as I strolled and pondered what my next move would be.

The ride to Trenton was perhaps 20 minutes and when I exited onto the platform waiting for the train, I felt like David Janssen who played Richard Kimble in 'The Fugitive'. For those not familiar with that storyline, 'Kimble' was on the run for 4 years after escaping a derailed train while on the way to the death house following a conviction for murdering his wife. When he finally secured his freedom after catching the one-armed man who actually did the killing, he walked the streets as a free man but couldn't avoid flinching when a police car pulled up in front of him.

Those officers were not there to arrest him, but to enter the courthouse where his sentence had just been vacated. In my case, having run from police and evading discovery for 30 days in the late summer of the previous year, it occurred to me that I was a free man and now that I was back in the States, I too…didn't have to run anymore.

After boarding the train, and looking out the window as the miles peeled away, it did not occur to me that all I had was the clothes on my back. No money. No job. No immediate prospects of finding one. No girl (that one still stung a bit as one might imagine). No specific plan. None of that mattered in the moment of that Friday afternoon. I was free and opportunity lay before me.

The train pulled into Baltimore City. I stepped off the passenger car and up the stairs to street level. Walking over to St. Paul Street and waiting on a corner to catch a bus, there I stood looking around at the downtown Baltimore skyline. The town felt like an old friend. There were no welcome home banners, not that I deserved or expected any. Nevertheless, it was a special feeling.

Boarding the number 3 bus for Halethorpe, I exited about 30 minutes later at the corner of Wilkens Avenue and Brunswick Street. Immediately I saw a couple of friends who recognized me. One said hello and asked if I was home on leave. I told him, 'Yes. For a long time.'

Moments later, I climbed the steps at 506 Brunswick Street and walked into the house. Both Mom and Dad were there. Mom enthusiastically welcomed me home. Dad, ever the practical one, said, 'Boy, you know you need to find a job'

Says I, 'Yes I know. I will be collecting unemployment for a while so I'll be okay for a time.' Dad replied, 'What are your plans? The answer? 'Radio. It's all I ever wanted, and that's what I will be doing'

Man, was it good to be home.

Me and Elaine. She be the lovely wife.

CHAPTER TWENTY-SIX

EPILOGUE

The spring and summer of 1976 was one of transition and preparation. There were two major forces in my world in that period. One was my continuing passion to enter the broadcasting business, and at the same time, I was lolling away the days and months living irresponsibly. Activities included tavern hopping, attending drinking parties, and coming and going as I pleased. God was merciful in delivering me through a lot of dicey situations.

Several weeks after I arrived at home, it was decided to look into studying at the Broadcasting Institute of Maryland. Owner John Jeppi and Admissions Director Steve Donahue invited me to come over to the school for a meeting and to take a tour of the facilities. Because of the mentorship of Captain Gregory Clark at Incirlik resisting a superior's determination to discharge me under less than full honorable conditions, I had complete funding under the G.I. Bill to pay for schooling at BIM. So, I signed up.

Meanwhile, I auditioned for a part time opening at radio station WITH. Having no experience, Program Director Ed Graham invited me in to take a crack at the slot and record a tape reading news copy and a couple of commercial scripts.

To say I was raw sounding and as green as the hills is an understatement. Ed finally told me after I persistently pestered him, 'You're not experienced enough, but keep working and maybe one day you'll get hired'.

Ed was reminded of that when he and I worked together some 20 years later at where else? WITH. In typical Graham humor, he said, 'Well, it took you awhile but here you are.'

I began attending the Institute in September 1976. It was a tremendously positive experience. My teachers were local broadcast icons who I grew up with. People like Dennis Hill, Bill LeFevre, George Lewis, Ernie Boston, and Wayne Gruehn. Guest speakers provided additional insight and inspiration like Jack Edwards and Chuck Richards. A few of these guys would later become co-workers and valued friends.

The school's disciplined and proven formula of hands-on writing, recording, and practice, practice, practice more than solidified in my mind the fact that my departing the Air Force was the right way to go.

It was in early February of 1977 that I was sent on an audition with two other classmates to radio station WSUX-FM (as in Sussex County). We each interviewed for a part-time weekend opening. We carpooled from Baltimore to Delaware that day. A bitterly cold day. So cold, that we drove over the Chesapeake Bay Bridge and looked out over a frozen solid bay.

Later that day after arriving home, a call came in. Mom answered it and handed the phone to me. 'Al Frazier from W-S-U-X'. With anticipatory excitement, I said hello and Al replied, 'I guess you know why I am calling? The job pays two dollars and twenty-five cents an hour and covers Saturday 5 PM to Midnight and Sunday 11AM to 5 PM. If you want it, it's yours.'

He could have offered me fifty cents an hour and I would have unhesitatingly said yes. I was the first student placed in a job from the

BIM class of 1976-77. I didn't show up much around the school after getting placed but did return for the Graduation in May that featured TV news anchor Sue Simmons as the Keynote Speaker.

I went full time at WSUX in June hosting the all-night show. Al Frazier, known as 'Big Al Frazier', was of inestimable help in leading me through a very undisciplined lifestyle during those days, working patiently with me and always taking time to talk radio and teach me a few things. He remains a dear friend of mine today.

Old radio guys never go away. There are too many good stories to tell from back in the day.

My ambition was to someday work in my hometown of Baltimore. That goal was attained in January 1979 when at the tender age of 21 years and one month, I landed a weekend position at Country FM 93.1 WPOC. A big station in a big town.

Once more, it was another Program Director who worked with me as a project. His name was Larry Clark. He was a noted Top 40 jock in markets like Pittsburgh, Cincinnati, and Cleveland. Now he had embraced Country at WPOC and was a master at incorporating the elements of pop hit radio into a Country sound. This all could not have come at a better time, as Country by the end of the 70's thanks to blockbuster movies like 'Urban Cowboy' and 'Every Which Way But Loose' were seeing pop audiences move over to stations like WPOC.

On the 10th of February 1979, which by the way fell on a Saturday that year, I marked a very significant anniversary. It was exactly four years before that I entered the Air Force. Had I served the full terms of my enlistment, that day would have been my exit from the military. But because my stint totaled 13 months, the time that would have been spent in the Air Force was instead applied to schooling, entering broadcasting, and working my way through two smaller stations to make it to a 50,000-watt Major Market FM which is where I was on that day. In a Baltimore radio studio doing a show.

1975: An Incredible Journey

My personal life during this time was very volatile and focused on one thing. Broadcasting. A feeble attempt at rekindling the relationship with Muriel in the Spring of 1976 went nowhere. Over the next few years I met several very nice girls but I was not settled down enough to even have a chance of becoming relationship material.

It has been 50 years since the events of his odyssey began to unfold. Time marches on. When I went through the year of 1975, none of the six members of my immediate family had a personal relationship with Jesus Christ. In the years to come, all six made professions of faith and served the Lord in various ways. Four have gone home to be with Him. Walt and Lynda left in 2023. Mom in 2007, and Dad who was the last to come to faith in Jesus during the summer of 1986, was the first to go the following year.

That leaves Gail and I. We both look forward to seeing the rest of the family again and we kid each other about who will be the last one to go. I told her she will. She says I will. Neither of us knows, but the Lord does.

The Lord knows many things. In fact, He says, 'Before I formed you in the womb I knew you'. He also knows the number of our days and also has a plan for each of us.

I'm in my mid-60's and have come to accept that most of my sand has already passed through the hourglass. Our time on earth is but for a season. God says our life is but a vapor. He exhorts us to lay up treasures (our priorities, actions, and time) with Heaven in mind. Pursuing the things of the world are futile. They in and of themselves will never satisfy, and in the end, they stay behind while we go on into eternity.

As I look back over those days of 1975, I have reunited with several of the people from that time. Air Force colleague Earl Hazelwood and I had a nice reunion by phone a couple of years ago. Al Frazier and I met up at a WSUX reunion in 2005 and again in 2020.

Jimmy Faris and I got together awhile back. The Thomas boys have also remained a constant source of friendship all along.

During these years my walk with Jesus has been fraught with trials and temptations, a number of which I brought on myself. Pride is a destructive trait and one of many things I have learned (and continue to learn) over the years is that having a humble and accepting spirit that yields to the Lord produces great joy and contentment.

No longer does one who made big mistakes need to beat himself or herself up about it. The devil will always delight in ambushing your conscience or memory with a thought or encounter to bring you down. The Lord says, 'Come unto Me all you who labor and are heavy laden, and I will give you rest'

It is my strengthening conviction that Christ is the best person to take your troubles to. He is God who took on the form of man, became the perfect sacrifice for our sins, and when you go to Him and tell Him you want to thank Him for doing that and that you want Him to apply that sacrifice and save and forgive you from yours…you need not ever bring them up again.

God doesn't. Why should you?

This journalistic effort was undertaken over a three-year period. There was no need to rush as I encountered people who I hadn't seen since those days who provided me with stories and insight that embellished the tale which you have read.

Which leads me to another point about the Lord. His timing. Even the arrival of Jesus as related in the New Testament book of Galatians 4:4 had everything to do with timing. Not a minute too soon, or too late. It is my observation that a person can be close to Christ and in a personal relationship for 75 years or more and still have room to grow as a person.

Maybe you're reading this book and you don't have a relationship with Christ. Maybe this book is planting a seed that brings you closer to His timing for you to become His child. And that is the way we have to come to Him. With the faith of a child.

A church won't save you. Church rules won't save you. It's impossible to live a sinless life so don't even try. The bible says that none of us are 'good'. Just keep this one fact in mind.

It's not that we are good people looking to become better. It's that we are sinful people who need to be forgiven. Nobody has to teach a child to do wrong. It's natural. Because we are born into sin. The person who dies with sins unforgiven goes to Hell for eternity. The person who dies with sins forgiven through what Christ did on the cross goes to Heaven. It's that simple. An either or. Only one can judge your soul. That is the Lord Jesus Christ.

When you take that step of faith and tell Christ that you are a sinner, that you recognize He went to the cross to die for your sins, and then ask Him to by faith and His word…hear your prayer, come into your heart, and forgive you of your sins, the Bible says you will have eternal life and will never see death.

To be absent from the body is to be present with the Lord. When you invite Him into your life? When you hear that still voice tugging at your heart, heed the call and put your hand in His. You will never ever regret that decision.

And then there is Muriel. You didn't think I'd leave off without a postscript, did you?

We reunited in 1989 for the purpose of me telling her I was now a believer in Christ as my Savior and wanted her to forgive me for anything I did from that 1975 period. From that time forward, we have stayed in touch. Never did we resume a romantic relationship but the love that was there 50 years ago turned into a solid friendship.

She has gone through the loss of two children and like all of us, has made decisions that were not in her best interests or in the interest of others. Today she lives a quiet life and spends time with her family members.

A few years back when discussing our breakup back in 1975, it was agreed that the $115.00 I sent home to her that was spent in a night of excess (remember, $115 bought a lot in 1975) convinced her to break it off, feeling I was too self-centered to care about what that money represented at the time. Building for a future that in her eyes at the time, I just threw away.

So, a good while ago, she received a card in the mail. Upon opening it, something fell out of the card and landed on the floor. She picked it up and read the following….

'It's been 50 years, but I told you I'd replace this and I am good to my word'.

It was cash totaling $115.

Which closes that chapter…and with that…closes this book.

I hope you enjoyed reading my little tale. May the Lord bless you and may you find peace in the Lord. Have a beautiful life!

ABOUT THE AUTHOR

Bob Mathers is a 50-year veteran of broadcasting. He has worked in all facets of the industry. His resume includes time in radio station ownership and management, decades of experience as an air personality and news anchor, and has also served as an advertising salesperson and commercial production writer and voice talent.

Bob regularly serves as Master of Ceremonies at various events and is known for his Public Speaking abilities. He also has taught broadcasting at accredited schools.

Today he oversees two internet radio stations that were launched a number of years ago. Ultimate Oldies Radio and German American Radio.

1975: An Incredible Journey is Mathers' second book. He also wrote the historical paperback '2012: The Year of Zillbilly and the Orioles'.

Bob resides in south central Pennsylvania with his wife Elaine and daughter (his precious Golden Doodle) Amber.